TABLE OF CONTENTS

No table of contents entries found.

PREFACE

I'm so glad you opened this book, it means you're really interested in online trading.

The opportunities are ever greater, the market is growing at a very good pace and we need as many people with initiative as possible, who want to take advantage of this trend.

I know, however, that the first steps are made difficult by the lack of information.

Ultimate eCommerce Masterplan - Nistor Zsolt

project media
simply amazing

Tens of thousands of entrepreneurs have started online businesses in Romania in recent years, many of them successfully, but although they had the advantage of starting early, it was a very difficult road for all of them - they had nowhere to learn, no one to turn to for information, the market was in its infancy, and so was the ecosystem necessary for the industry (hosting companies, eCommerce platforms, marketing agencies, courier companies, etc.).

Things have changed in recent years, commerce is moving faster and faster to the Internet and the entire economy is becoming digital. In other words, you are entering this industry at a great time!

From the point of view of the information needed to build an online business, a lot of it is now publicly available. It is difficult, however, to find and choose credible sources, especially when you have so many things to do, as is the case at the beginning of any business.

Well, the book you are holding in your hand contains everything you need to know if you want to build an online business.

By reading it, you will gain many years of experience in entrepreneurship and online commerce.

Regardless of whether or not you have experience online or in commerce, you will find here answers to all important questions, plus clear recipes for all important aspects when building your business online.

Although it is easy to read, it is not an easy book. I recommend that you go through it carefully, having a notebook and a pen next to you. I guarantee that many ideas will come to you, and at the end of it you will have all the information to start an online business.

I will take you through the commercial, legal, technical, marketing and HR aspects, logistics, etc., and will do all this in a friendly and accessible language, explaining, however, concepts that are often very complex. Now is the time to end the preface and get down to business.

"This is the best advice I can give you, wait and dream and continue even if there are problems or obstacles. If you're ready, you have a plan, it's insurmountable." On the course of the journey cooked, you have a plan and you are motivated, no obstacle start as soon as possible, don't rush, inevitably they will appear

GOOD LUCK!

HOW TO READ THIS BOOK

When you want to do something, you immediately take action. For most of us, the first step is education. The action taken in step two is for those who want success.

Because I know about a lot of challenges and problems that entrepreneurs have when it comes to eCommerce, I chose to put on paper - this time - the stories through which I managed to move forward.

What's more, in addition to the experiences we had in the market, in this book you will discover a lot of examples and ideas that we realized together with the team for our clients.

If you find yourself reading these lines, you 100% have an interest in eCommerce and want to understand more or validate your knowledge.

From my point of view, you now have more than a book in your hand. You have a mentor who will help you every step of the way.

How to read the book and come out 100% winning at the end

More often than not, attention to detail makes the difference, both in business and in personal life.

So my suggestion is to be as proactive as possible when going through this book. Take notes on ideas that apply to your plan, underlining or bulletin the information of greatest interest.

Before you go any further, make sure you have a sheet of paper and a pencil or pen with you.

At the end of the book you have an eCommerce dictionary, in alphabetical order. If you come across terms you don't understand in the book, check the dictionary - it will help.

Ultimate eCommerce Masterplan - Nistor Zsolt

BEGINNINGS

My first contact with technology was with arcade games. I was crazy about them, I would sit for hours and spend all my money just to play them. The arcade was near my grandmother and I remember going there every weekend just to be close to the arcade and play.

In the end, the owner of the hall made some changes and brought some computers, probably to test whether they would show interest or not. He couldn't even imagine that all the kids had moved from Arcade games to PCs.

In a short time, he removed all the games and replaced them with PCs, thus transforming the Arcade game room into the first PC club în Timișoara. My money went from Arcade games to PC games. Again I sat for hours fascinated by absolutely all the games, whether it was Supaplex, Doom, Red Alert, Warcraft, etc.

The passion for PCs continued and after a few years I had my first PC. After a short time I had the first modem with which I could connect to the Internet.

GAME CHANGER!!!

Although for a kid, the biggest joy was not access to a bunch of information, but rather the ability to download music, I was in ninth heaven.

As the years went by, I discovered more and more about the internet and was somewhat fascinated by the websites I was browsing, so much so that one day, together with some friends, we decided to start making websites.

We didn't even start, because they gave up on the idea, but the idea that I could create websites remained imprinted on me, and that's how I started reading as much as possible about web design, html, css, editing photo, etc.

Later I opened my own agency and continued my passion for making websites, but this time also for money. I have created many websites, including many online stores. I remember one of the online stores I did, it's a veterinary product store that in the first months after launch had an average of 50 visitors per month, and which now (7 years later) has sales of over 10,000 euros/month.

After that came other stores and other results (some good, some bad), but somehow at some point I discovered a series of procedures that I had been implementing without realizing it, until recently, when it came to creating and launching an online store.

Now, about you

If you picked up this book, it means that you are ready to launch your own project and want to propel it to the top. Honestly, I'm happy for you. You have managed to get rid of the limits, measure your risks and you are ready to create something that will change your life and the lives of others around you.

That's why I'm here. To help you lay brick by brick and create something impressive.

In almost 15 years of work, I have helped launch hundreds of successful businesses, starting in college with creating the first official website for a coffee shop. Even though you may not find it very interesting, it changed my life. And it made me realize something.

If you want something with all your conviction and are willing to fight, don't give up even if everyone seems to be standing in your way... you will win.

Now it seems impossible for me to imagine what my life would look like if I hadn't started my own business.

It's a huge feeling of power and freedom when you're your own boss and in control of your own future. And that's not necessarily about money you make or the car you own. Nor the fact that you can sit on the beach and drink cocktails all day long and bask in the sun.

Every day, you have the chance to transform the lives of your customers and see how, thanks to you, things change for the better. You have the chance to enjoy more time with your family and loved ones and do things that a standard schedule from 8 to 4 would never allow you to do.

I know you have dreams and goals too. Otherwise you wouldn't be reading this book.

Something inside you motivates you to look for the best way to achieve your goals and bring your dreams to life. You can already imagine the comfort, pleasure, safety and pride of having your own business - your own online store.

But how do you get there?

You have information, because libraries, the Internet and your entourage en: of them. But you also need a system, a recipe to guide you step by step towards your destination.

Let me be your guide on this journey. This is also the reason why I wrote this book - to help you find your best path and correctly visualize the steps you have to take along the way.

The Pandemic

It changed and broke a lot of businesses and business concepts. On a global level, the effects are devastating, but for the e-commerce part, honestly, it was the best growth accelerator.

Together with my team, we had the chance to be present in the front line, to see the impact on the economy. The most important thing is to see the decisions and actions of entrepreneurs affected by these changes.

Now it has been confirmed, once again, how much technology helps in the development of humanity - the fact that many things can be done differently than we were used to. I am referring to the way of working remotely, which has taken off. For many it has become a normality.

The socializing, educating and networking part of people that happens at various offline events has moved online enabling more individuals to access such information, now a click away.

And trade, do you think it has remained the same? Both you and I and everyone we know have different needs, desires and aspirations. There are things we need to survive, and things simply for our pleasure, or for pride.

This was the moment when e-commerce exploded, when people had to make all these purchases online, from online stores. And guess what, many experienced entrepreneurs, especially young ones, saw the opportunity and acted very quickly.

I have been online since 2000. I have seen and done many interesting things, but what I have seen during this time has been incredible. If someone had told me about these numbers and increases, I wouldn't have believed them.

For example, I launched an online specialty coffee shop that generated sales of 20,000 Euros in the first 6 months, or a swimming pool construction business site that generated leads of over 80,000 Euros in the first year after launch.

Step by step towards what you want

I won't lie to you. I'm a pragmatic person with a technical background, so what I write is rarely inspirational. Rather, they are 100% working, tested formulas that help you get from point A to point B successfully, without additional blah-blahs. If you want to keep dreaming, make lists of your dreams, find your mantra and open your inner eye or I know some mystical stuff, this book is not the best for you.

But if you want an online store that will sell from day one, bring you financial security and the satisfaction of shaping your own future, then don't put it down until you reach the last page. It will help you find the answers you are looking for.

I have divided the book into 5 main chapters in the logical order of building a business. We start with planning and how to find your own business model.

Then we step through the stages of creation, launch and growth where I will also give you advanced marketing tips. The last chapter is about automating your business so you can save even more time to enjoy what really matters to you.

Again, this is not an easy book.

But it's a recipe book, a manual that you should keep with you all the time and that you can consult with confidence at every stage of building your business.

They are recipes based on which I have launched hundreds of successful businesses and which sell tens of thousands of euros daily.

Are you ready?

Let's take the first step in the journey of your life.

DO YOU WANT TO CONQUER THE WORLD? YOU NEED A PLAN!

Why?
Behind every decision there is a motivation. Everything starts from this "why": a personal change, a relationship, a business.

Before you go through all the steps that the book you are holding in front of you will guide you through, I want to give you some evidence why it is worth selling online in your own store, starting today.

So why (have your own online store)?

Over 5.6 billion euros (according to GPC). Growth of up to 10.87 trillion dollars by 2025. The largest percentage growth of e-commerce, with more than 27% (Ecommerce Europe & Statista).

eCommerce is growing day by day, from click to click.

Why make a store as soon as possible?

Because it's simpler, faster and cheaper. And because it's safer, you have more options and no barriers related to location or time.

Too little said? I thought so.

Let's take them one at a time, but be careful, I wouldn't want you to completely rule out the idea of a physical presence in addition to the online one, sometime later when you grow up or even now, if you already have an offline business and just started thinking of selling online

First of all, an online store is cheaper than the entire investment you would have to make in a physical store, including inventory, location, employees, and so on. Online, you can sell alone (in the beginning), without having any product in stock, and in terms of location... You can sell absolutely anywhere as long as you have the internet. eCommerce is breaking all boundaries. Put yourself in the shoes of your future client or hey, you may have found yourself in this situation often.

If he wants to buy a product at a physical location, first he has to get ready to leave the house (maybe in his pajamas), drive to the store (maybe fill up with gas), find a place to parking lot (and this is when he goes out of his mind), look for the product on the shelf, stand in line to pay for it, and then drive back home.

Ultimate eCommerce Masterplan - Nistor Zsolt

Online, your customer can stay in their pajamas and find the product more easily, buy it and wait for it to arrive directly at their door. Much simpler, isn't it?

And even if you are the one who makes sure that the whole process remains comfortable for the customer, it is also easier for you.

You are more visible online

Today the eCommerce market provides you with a lot of solutions that help you launch your store quickly, without hassles regarding the technical side or marketing or customer loyalty or anything. So it gives you the time you need to take care of the store and orders.

Because, as you may already know, a business of any type requires two main investments: time and money. Being a startup, many entrepreneurs don't have extravagant funds - but that's not a problem when you go online.

Why? Think about how many people you can reach online compared to the customers of a physical store. Let's see a practical example.

Let's say you want an online store with various birthday gifts. By default, this means that people will search for you on anniversaries - birthdays, name anniversaries, wedding anniversaries, etc.

Good and let's see the second option. Instead of being online, you have a physical store in the Timisoara sector for example. How much audience do you think you have when you're offline? Out of over 300,000 inhabitants of the city; less than 5% will buy from you on an anniversary. Because they don't know about you. And they don't feel like going all the way across town to find you.

WHY HAVE AN ONLINE STORE?

But online, people from all over the country and even from abroad will buy your products, every day - with the right strategy.

This without taking into account that when you sell in a physical location, you depend on the schedule. You have a schedule and no matter how long it is, sooner or later you have to close the house and go to sleep. Instead, online, your site continues to work around the clock, and if people feel like ordering at 12 at night, the orders will be waiting for you in the admin in the morning.

If I haven't convinced you yet, I'll show you a few more that will surely do the job for me. According to Google, over 40% of customers prefer to research products before buying them, and over 40% of customers compare 3 or more sites before making a purchase.

Online is the place where you can turn your idea into reality and not only that: you can sell as much as you want and need, to achieve financial security, a comfortable living and a lifestyle the way you want it. To get there, you need a plan and a lot of work. I'm not going to lie to you, the book you're reading now requires ambition and a lot of determination on your part. My advice is to keep it close at every step of creating your own business because it will help you enormously - it will be a framework that, once applied, is guaranteed to get you where you want to go.

TYPES OF ONLINE BUSINESSES

In case when you picked up the book in your hand, you surely skimmed through it and noticed that I focus strictly on the process of creating a full-fledged online store. But the store is not the only way to sell online in the long term, nor the only channel you can use once.

Although there are some parallels in the physical world, the beauty of online is the ease with which you have access to the same audience, regardless of the size of your business.

Physically, a small island attached to Iulius Mall în Timișoara has no way of having a higher visibility (implicitly an audience) than a blog that promotes the same type of products online. The same is the case with a physical mall or even the market where grandma goes to sell her greens, as the equivalent of malls and online marketplaces

Going back to the idea before, there are a multitude of methods to sell online and I will introduce you to the most popular ones.

Selling online

Ultimate eCommerce Masterplan - Nistor Zsolt

The first and, in my personal opinion, the most serious type of online business is selling through an online store, regardless of whether we are talking about B2B (business to business) or B2C (business to customer). Imagine that the online store is practically your house, from the foundation to the roof, from the upholstered sofa in the living room to the lavender pots you have strung on the balcony. No one will come to kick you out of your house or impose rules on you. You just have to pay your bills (hosting, etc.) and taxes, and the house (website) will work great.

The online store concept is not just milk and honey. There are advantages and disadvantages, the most common of which relates to cost.

You can't build an online store for free. But you can greatly reduce costs depending on the choices you make.

You can work with your own stocks or do dropshipping. You can invest more or less in certain marketing channels. You can choose an eCommerce solution with all the functionalities you need natively, in the platform, or you can use other platforms, open source or not, but at that moment you have to think carefully if you want to be a programmer, to deal with the changes yourself in code, third-party integrations and plugins (the most effective being paid ones).

Or you want to be an entrepreneur and sell.

I'll stop here for now because you'll get all the details of what it means to sell in an online store throughout the entire book.

Selling on a marketplace

eMAG, Doraly, Amazon and many others represent the concept of a marketplace, a platform that, in addition to its own products, also offers other sellers the opportunity to display their product catalog - for a fee.

So, another way to sell your products is through a marketplace, a platform that comes with both advantages and disadvantages. Many entrepreneurs choose to test their business idea by starting with selling on the marketplace (for example, selling handmade products on Breslo and then creating a stand-alone online boutique) or treat it as an additional sales channel when the company develops sufficiently. Either approach is correct.

The strong points of a marketplace are the low start-up costs, the presentation on an existing infrastructure, already known to the public and the fact that you benefit directly from the strong marketing done by the team behind it.

I think the weaknesses are obvious: you have fierce competition, few customers are aware that they are ordering from you, not from the marketplace itself, you have no way to assert your brand and you have no access to your customer base. Plus the commissions and rules you're bound to follow.

Selling on a blog

Earning money from blogging is not impossible, but it's not as easy as all the sites you find when you search for *"how to make money online"* make it out to be. Basically no, you can't just lie back on your sun lounger in the Maldives and wait for the money to flow.

Out of over 95,000 blogs at last count (according to Zelist), only a small percentage of owners can boast that they actually make a living from blogging alone. Even fewer are influencers.

To sell, realistically speaking, with the help of a blog, you first need a period of time and a lot of content to create a community around it, to gather a base of loyal readers and email addresses.

On the blog you can sell physical products through shopping buttons, you can affiliate, write advertisements, offer consulting services, information, etc.

The idea is that regardless of what you want to sell, you need a loyal audience to address and whose attention must be constantly maintained, similar to the case when you have an online store.

Selling on an AD Platform

eBay, OLX, craigslist.com, okazii.ro, publi24.ro, etc. You've surely heard of at least one of the classifieds sites I've mentioned by now. In principle, this type of sale does not fit into the concept of a serious business plus, with repeated sales with a large total profit without declaring it, you have legal problems.

Now, I'm not telling you not to sell on classifieds sites at all. At least in the beginning, it's a good way to test the market, outline a suitable price for your products and identify a typology of customers to address. But as we said before, the legal "business" on classified sites is not really an online business.

A Presentation Website

In presentation sites you can present your services and allow potential customers to ask you for a personalized offer (or not) for their specific needs.

If you don't sell physical products - you don't need a shopping cart - a showcase site is a suitable solution for your kind of online sale. Practically, in such a site you can advertise a lot of types of services: photo-video, event organization, hotel services, art, legal services, dentistry, cosmetic offices, hairstyling services, etc.

Well, even if you don't have an eCommerce platform behind you, you shouldn't underestimate the workload for a "simple" presentation site, and especially for its promotion. And hence the related costs.

Yes, you can go to the boy next door who knows how to play with a theme on a free platform, but you will have a fixed site for what you paid for it. Remember that your website requires programming, design, usability, optimization, SEO, etc., you can't just jump out of bed one morning and shout *"I want a website too! That's it, I'm doing it today!"*.

Imagine leaving your entire business in the hands of the boy next door who makes your website. Does that sound scary? Then why would you want to make your website with him? If your goal is to have a showcase website and sell your services through it, make sure the way it looks and behaves also defines the quality of your work - it needs to load quickly, look great and meet the needs of your potential customers.

Keep all these things in mind and choose your partners very carefully, if necessary to build your website.

BUSINESS MODEL

In the past, business was undeniably much simpler: you produced something and sold it for a profit, quickly building a reputation and a loyal clientele that was passed down from father to son. Before the industrial revolution, most sales were done locally - competition was minimal, demand was usually maximum, and you set the price as you pleased.

Fast forward, today you live and sell in an ocean full of sharks. You're fighting with competing firms globally, and besides the fact that you have to be super creative to reach customers, they're hard to please.

In this context, without a plan and a business model, you have no chance. There is a clear connection between a business plan and a model, the former being actually the advanced version of the business model.

In short, the business model outlines how you will create, deliver and capture value. It explains what consumer pain points you choose to cure, why your solution works better than the competition's, and what balance exists between what the customer wants to pay and the costs you have to bear.

Think of the business model as if it were a car. Different parts work differently - for example, a conventional engine runs differently than a hybrid engine, a standard transmission is different than an automatic transmission - therefore creating different value for drivers.

The way the car was built - the business - indicates certain signals for what the driver can do and determines the maneuvers he uses. One of the most stable and effective templates on which to create your own business model was designed by Alex Osterwalder in 2008. Today there are hundreds of sites and tools that allow you to establish the model in less than 20 minutes, without stocking up on paper and pens.

Who do you want to sell to: client segmentation

In the beginning it was the customer. And in the middle and at the end.

You see, without customers you can't sell, and if you don't satisfy them, your business idea goes down the drain. Customers are the heart of every business - the moment they stop buying, the business dies.

Why do you need to establish several customer segments from the start? Because at this point you have to be aware of which groups you can sell to, how, on which channels, what relationship to establish with each one - including whether you want to serve them or want to ignore them.

Customer groups represent segments if their needs justify a different offer for each of them, if they are approached through different communication channels, if they need a different type of relationship, if they want to pay differently for various extra services, etc.

Basically, you can directly address the mass, a huge group of consumer segments with similar needs and requirements, but to whom you address with different value propositions, communication channels and type of relationship.

Another type of segment is represented by niche consumers - an audience that you can reach more easily and quickly because everything related to your business model becomes specific to the chosen niche.

They, in turn, can be segmented.

Consumers can then be diversified into two or more segments - Amazon is a telling enough example, the categories of products sold dictate the variety of segments to which it sells.

And we also have multiple markets with the example of online newspapers: on the one hand, they address readers directly, inviting them to buy subscriptions, and on the other hand, they attract advertisers to display their desired ads.

What's your value proposition

What do you and only you offer consumers? How do you differentiate yourself from the existing competition on the market? What value do you bring to the lives of your customers?

Establish a unique value proposition and you will know from the start how you want to position yourself on the market. All the materials you will use in creating and promoting your business will start from this.

The value proposition satisfies a need or solves a problem for a consumer. Here you have two possibilities: either you offer something innovative, something new, or you launch with an offer similar to those on the market, but with something extra that no one else has.

So, what do you offer customers: novelty, customization possibilities, a better price, lower risks, consulting, partnerships, a more accessible product / service?

Think carefully about your business idea and find out what you bring new or extra to the market for customers. But be careful, don't fall into the trap of your own ego: even if you are passionate about your business idea and you know it helps you, personally, research thoroughly if it also helps others. Especially those who have something to pay you with.

Choosing distribution channels

As many as possible, right?

Totally wrong. In the beginning, we all feel the urge to think big, we all want a lot. We want to surround our prey knowing that sooner or later it will fall. But we forget how many resources we lose on the way for a prey that may not even taste good.

I say this with the idea that you can approach the potential customer on all available channels, investing time, money, employees - a ton of resources - only to have them return the product, be dissatisfied and complain all over the place, destroying the image of the brand or other bad result.

When choosing the channels for your business model, you have several standards at your disposal. You can sell in your own store or outlet, you can use partner channels (for example, distributors) or you can do a combination of the two - that's how dropshipping works.

Obviously, you can use a mix of channels to present your products, but don't forget for a moment that they involve the customer passing through different phases, starting with his familiarization with your brand, evaluation, the moment of purchase and up to delivery and after-sales strategy.

The way to maintain the relationship with customers

Has it ever happened to you to enter a store and be approached before you cross the threshold with the formula *"Can I help you with something?"* Oh, almost all the time?

Ok, it's time to get rid of the theory of the helpless, blind and idiot customer.

Your goal is to maintain a mutually beneficial relationship with each individual client for the long term - as cliche as that sounds. The sale is not reduced to the product added to the cart and delivered, done, goodbye.

On the other hand, there are different ways in which the client relationship proceeds. It can be personal assistance - based on human interaction, even personal assistance dedicated to each customer in a more special way, self-service, automated services, community or co-creation (for example, Facebook).

Income stream

The revenue stream is the cash your business generates from each customer segment. The question is what value are consumers really willing to pay for? What and how do I currently pay? Or how would they prefer to pay?

The answers to the previous questions will help you identify including payment methods for your future online project so document yourself well.

Basically, there are 7 major types of income: sale of assets (direct sale of products and services), subscription fee, commission (real estate agencies), rental (see Uber, Airbnb), sale of license (film production, copyright) , payment for the right of use (hotels, guesthouses, telephone services) and advertising.

Moreover, depending on the type of income stream, you can establish different price mechanisms, fixed or dynamic, starting from list price, price dependent on functionality, price per volume or customer segment, up to negotiation or auction.

So, answer the following questions:

How does your product or service generate revenue?

Who pays you? The consumer, another business, a licensee, etc.?

How do you set prices? Price per unit, transaction fee, etc.?

When do you get paid? How do you get the money? Immediately, after a certain period of time, etc.?

What is your pricing model?

What is the lifetime value of each customer? Annual revenue multiplied by the number of years the customer will continue to pay you.

Is the revenue stream model scalable? Can you respond to a sudden increase in sales without exhausting your resources?

Key resources

Resources are products, people, and collaborators, elements that your company uses to create the value proposition, serve the consumer segment, and deliver the products or services to customers.

In this block of the business model you need to identify the key resources you need to keep the promise of the value proposition, but also for distribution channels, customer relationship and revenue streams.

And here applies the saying to have with whom, but also to have with what. In other words, your key resources are both human - your employee or team, including you - and financial, physical and/or intellectual. See if you can afford to work alone or if you want to hire internal people, outsource to a freelancer or an agency.

Key activities

Like key resources, activities must create and deliver a unique value proposition, maintain customer relationships, reach consumer segments, and earn revenue. Now is the time to ask yourself what activities you have to do for all the other blocks we discussed earlier.

For example, the typical activities for an online store can be documentation, production, marketing, logistics, packaging and sales, with all the secondary activities that derive from this.

Who are your key partners and how do you choose them

Tell me who you're friends with, so I can tell you who you are. A correctly chosen partner can take you to the heights and help you maintain the relationship with the customer segments.

When creating the business model, think about who your partners are or could be. In this case, partners start from product, hosting and platform providers and continue to courier companies, payment processors, influencers, etc.

Now, before you choose a partner, think about the following: create a clear contract / understandable for both parties, define expectations from each party, assess the impact this partnership could have on your customers, and follow the rule of thumb reciprocal.

The types of partnerships you can enter into are strategic alliances with a non-competing firm, strategic alliances with competition, affiliation with a company to create new businesses, and buyer-supplier relationships.

Why enter into partnerships? Simple, because that's how you have the opportunity to make economies of scale or you can greatly reduce certain risks or you can offer something extra to customers, which differentiates you and motivates them to buy.

COSTS, INVESTMENTS & FUNDS

We intentionally ignored a vital building block of the business model - the cost structure. This is for the simple reason that the elements related to the cost structure deserve an entire chapter.

I want you to understand: I know that to a lesser or greater extent you build a business because you want to make money, make a profit and stop worrying about tomorrow, at least from a financial point of view.

But money does not fall from the sky, no matter how much we would like it. Before you can make a profit, you need to invest money, know what cash flow means and how important it is, to understand the entire cost structure that an online business entails.

The costs of the business largely depend on its specifics and on the choices you make, but they increase in direct proportion to the volume of business growth. Do you hire one person or more before launching the store? Do you handle the store yourself or outsource to an agency / freelancer?

All of these determine the amount of costs you have to bear, regardless of whether they are fixed or variable. Or hidden.

Honestly, it amuses me how some people talk about the costs of an online business. Most limit the cost to the platform and/or marketing, forgetting about everything else.

Wrong. The costs that you are going to bear start from the expense of opening the company, licenses, activity space, utilities, maintenance and continue with insurance, stocks, losses of stocks, postponement of payment terms that puts your cash flow at risk (that that still happens), payment processor fees and your personal time.

Ok, you can tell me that you work from home, from your laptop or personal computer and work alone. If you open your business like this, do you think someone else will pay the electricity, water and property taxes? They also belong to you, and if you carry out the economic activity at the declared headquarters, the taxes increase up to 6-15 times or even more.

I don't want to discourage you by telling you all this, but it's vital to be terribly aware of everything that goes into creating an online store.

When creating your business model, write down all the costs you expect to incur, including your time.

Remember, over 90% of businesses go out of business in less than 3 years because they fail to understand the importance of the costs required to deliver the value proposition to the right customer segments.

BUSINESS PLAN

With a simple search on the internet you will find dozens of templates ready for any business plan, starting from the establishment of a walnut plantation to the creation of an online store, in any kind of niche.

Because I'm not going to reinvent the wheel for nothing, I'm going to show you some essential business

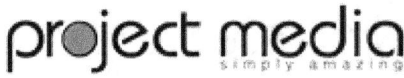

plan points that you can also find online. They are the same, yes, and reduced to a minimum because I never understood the point of writing 10-20 pages with all kinds of predictions, which you would be afraid to re-read.

Stop for a second. All you need is a short plan, based on the previously created business model, on the principle of K.I.S.S (Keep It Stupid Simple) - not a novel that no one reads (except when you are founding a corporation or looking for investors).

The business plan is a product in itself, so the first question you need to ask is who are you making it for. For you, as a founder, first of all, but also for investors, financial institutions, clients or suppliers, employees, etc.

In other words, first you determine how your business works, in detail, then you can use the data to create a pitch for an investor or a sales pitch for customers.

What does the business plan take from the business model? Everything but takes it to a higher level.

The Product

What product / service do you want to sell?
Write down the features and benefits of your product, where you are with its development (if applicable), the technology or technique used (if it helps you differentiate yourself from the competition), future products or services. However, don't get too excited about the string of features - neither now, in the plan, nor in the product description, on the site.

The customer is interested in whether your product solves a problem or covers a need, he doesn't care how many features it has. Because you can have the best product - if it doesn't help the customer, it's for nothing.

Also note here the differentiating elements from the competition and possibly what functionality will be sacrificed in your product compared to the competitors.

Consumers

Now that you have the product, who do you want to sell it to?

The simplest answer is found by following the problem you are solving with your solution / product. Who are the people facing this problem? What age, gender, behavior, personalities, interests do they have?

John is a 27-40 year old guy. John notices a girl he likes at a party, but... he doesn't go to greet her. John has the same problem that most of us have: he is afraid of being rejected.

The solution? He can create an account on a dating app / dating.com

Follow the same template to identify your target audience based on the problem. If you have already realized the business model, it is possible that you have already found not only one typology of consumers, but several segments.

The revenue stream model

We have already reviewed the essential information about the revenue stream for your business, but in the business plan you need to additionally analyze the macro environment as well as the trends.

Oh yes, you can't get a crystal ball to predict the future, but you have nothing to lose by trying to determine what types of changes could affect your business and in what way - positively or negatively.

Basically, the macro environment is composed of several major factors such as the economic environment, the political environment, the social environment, the legal environment, the environment and technology. For example, if you're launching a technology startup, it's clear that you need to follow technology trends with maximum attention. What is innovative and extraordinary today becomes obsolete tomorrow. Can you keep up?

Analyzing the macro environment may lead you to redo the product or some of its functionality to last in the long term. So don't hesitate to take into account the external elements that could affect your business.

How to analyze the market & the competition

What is the size of your target market? How are online sales going in this sector?

At this stage you do an analysis of the industry in which you are going to operate, including the analysis of competitors. Do you know what your competitors are doing? How satisfied are customers with their services and products? Do you know what your competitors' strategy is?

Obviously, no competitor will give you this information, but you can discover it in another way: see what marketing they do (see the posts on Facebook, what emails they send, what ads they present), buy their products and analyze them (including everything that happens from the moment of the order until after it is received), analyze the websites of competitors and, if possible, go to their stores and see how the employees behave.

But don't stop there: do an opinion survey among the competition's customers, see why they choose to buy there, what they comment about the competition, either good or bad. This way you will discover possible advantages for your own business or weak points to cover.

This is also the time to outline a general marketing plan for the launch of your project, noting the tactics of promotion, sale, potential partners (which you already have in the business model).

What you know how to do & what you choose to outsource

After you understand your product, market and target audience, it's time to identify the main skills that need to be developed within your company (or that you have to develop) so that you can deliver the promised value to customers.

Ultimate eCommerce Masterplan - Nistor Zsolt

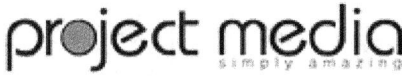

Analyze what skills you have, what qualities you need to develop and what you outsource.

I know both entrepreneurs who started out with a team, but I also know several who started alone and, as they evolved, hired other people.

At some point, when you keep developing, it's inevitable that you don't ask for help - you simply can't cope physically and mentally anymore.

Always keeping in mind the unique value proposition, first establish the brand culture, continuing with the responsibilities of the founder and the way of organization for the smooth functioning of the company.

The financial model & plan best fitted for you

In the business plan, financial forecasts are the easiest to overestimate given that you are juggling numbers that you cannot test beforehand. However, it is absolutely necessary to do the financial estimations and understand some terms so that you have control over your business.

An important aspect here is the financial objective (turnover, number of products sold) over a limited period of time. Why? Because without a lens it's like buying the most expensive GPS and... that's it.

You would never enter a destination.

Unlike the comparison with the GPS, your destination is not absolutely mandatory to reach, but it is ideal that at the end of the set period you are as close as possible to it. Write down your goal in currency/$, for the next 3-4 years in detail, but also a 5-year financial vision.

The first spending plan you make is related to the company's start-up budget - here you include the costs we discussed in the business model. Then comes the balance sheet estimate (assets - liabilities = equity), the break-even point calculation, the profit and loss estimate, and the cash flow estimate.

Cash flow is all the money that is generated and received by your business over a period of time.

To forecast cash flow, you need to identify the sources of income and when the money will come in versus understanding the costs and when they need to be covered.

It is vital to think about cash flow in the context of a multitude of factors, from operational costs such as rent or payroll, to seasonal fluctuations, stock turnover and cash on delivery payments.

The intervention plan

If something is going to go wrong, it will. And at the most inopportune moment. I don't say it, Murphy, *"the one with the laws"* says it. For this reason, it is preferable to have a plan B and C and to recognize the indicators that warn you that you are in a crisis situation.

Establish from the beginning the criteria by which you realize that your project is beginning to fall into the void, what are the measures to take to close the whole business, how much money you need and in what time you can liquidate the business.

Again, I don't want to discourage you, but in business you need lucidity and you have to be completely honest with yourself to make it work. You may end up in this situation, you may not, but a plan like this never hurts.

Once you've finalized your business plan, implement it immediately and stick to it. It is normal for the plan to undergo changes along the way, but not major changes that will turn everything upside down. And one more tip: you can calmly present it to a consultant, an accountant, etc., no one will steal your idea. Instead, you get an objective opinion to correct some mistakes or shortcomings.

Based on the business plan, you will practically build your own online business, from the organizational structure to the marketing plan, the financial model and so on.

CREATING AN ONLINE BUSINESS

and THEN THERE WAS LIGHT...THE IDEA

The first step is always the hardest. The same thing happens in business. Have you ever wondered how Larry Page came up with the idea for Google? Or Elon Musk to the idea of PayPal? From the outside, it may seem like pure magic or incredible luck, but in reality there are specific methods to arrive at a good business idea.

You see, some businesses are meant to stay. Restaurants, hotels, taxis, music. These are the businesses that have been with us - in one form or another - for hundreds of years. People need to eat and sleep and get from point A to point B. Universally, we all listen to music.

But, in addition to these necessary forms of business, there is a whole world of ideas that even in our imagination we would not consider "successful". And yet they sell.

So, the million euro question is how you find the idea and the business niche, but above all, how you execute it.

Some are lucky enough to come up with a brilliant idea from the start, or it is immediately solved by the specificity of the product - when you are the manufacturer, it is obvious that the business idea will be related to this product in one way or another.

Ideas are of many kinds: they can hit you unexpectedly, in any situation you are in, whether you are behind the wheel, in the shower, in a meeting, out with friends, etc.; they can come from within, from the desire to find a solution, a better solution to a problem you are facing, or you look for them deliberately, based on a process, starting from a motivation.

The system we'll discuss next helps you find an idea deliberately, even if you don't have one right now. Oh yeah, and don't use the *"I have no idea ok"* excuse.

We all have something special that we are unusually good at. Maybe you are good at training dogs or you have a very good sense for decorating a home so that it gives you the feeling of "home". Or maybe you're the one your friends are always asking to fix their computer.

If you want a business but don't have an idea yet, don't wait for it to magically come from somewhere in the stars. You rarely get an idea by thinking. You find it doing.

Let me now show you a system through which you reach the right idea for your own online business.

Why do you want a business?

Start with this. It's the perfect time to find your motivation (so you'll know how to tell anyone what motivated you to become a successful person).

Think about what situation you faced - what made you so ambitious to offer a better solution? What problem did you have? What did you want to do to make the world more comfortable, more pleasant, safer, more beautiful, etc., for you and others?

Your business ideas don't have to be completely innovative. They just have to be different from what we have on the market. There is only one Google, one Facebook and one Apple. But each of them started based on other products or services, none of them were the first on the market. They just did things differently.

Start by making a list and write first what your goal and motivation are. Write down business ideas starting from the identified motivation: do you want to offer parents with young children alternative toys for their intellectual development? Do you want people to feel completely safe in their own homes so you sell security systems?

You can detail the business idea from the start depending on the type of product (if you know it), the target audience, the type of business, etc.

Begin with a bad idea

Today's best lesson for you is yesterday's mistake.

Here's the coolest job when you're looking for a business idea. You have total freedom to be a cabbage, to come up with ideas that, whichever way you turn them, have no way of resisting or that simply sound crazy. Don't hesitate to write down everything that comes to your mind. Even if it doesn't stand a chance, don't worry - you will pass each idea through a filter, you will test it before you apply it.

I admit, before I just wanted to do - anything. I've had ideas that have given me a healthy boost before, based on which I've learned, but I've also had bad ideas.

I made mistakes and learned painfully expensive lessons. I learned from them how to test my ideas and how to figure out if they are worth it or not - so that I can tell you now what to avoid, so you don't go through the same situations.

But it all starts with this realization: in the beginning, in the prospecting phase, you have every right to be a cabbage. Once you realize that, move on.

What are you already paying for?

Now I want you to think about the things or activities that you are already paying someone else to do. Why? Because many are embarrassed at the idea that someone would pay them for something.

But if you think about it, we already pay others for what they make or sell, from food, interior decoration items, phone to cleaning, car oil change or tennis lessons.

Write down 5-10 things or activities on your list. When you start building your list, you'll notice that you're paying a lot of people every day. That's why I started with this question. It opens your mind, you see all the possibilities.

What can you do?

And besides, what do you like? The first customer of your business is you. What are you passionate about?

There are millions of businesses in the world created out of passion, and there's nothing wrong with that. Do you enjoy drinking tea, driving, shopping, organizing holidays, fishing, running, etc.? Very well, start writing down at least 10 such things that you like or are passionate about.

Also think about what experience/skills you have. Have you worked in a furniture store for 5 years? Why not open an online store in the same field, since you already know what the operational side entails, logistics, suppliers, types of customers, etc.?

Or were you a salesperson for a mobile accessories company? It means you already know the stocks, prices, customer preferences and so on. You also know specifications about each individual phone brand. So you can open an online accessories store, only with a certain type of accessories (e.g. covers) or a phone store.

Write down your skills and experience on the same list and let's move on.

What do your friends say you are good at?

Innate or learned skills become so natural to us that we often forget them.

Maybe your friends tell you that you always wear the coolest outfit or you give the best advice in sentimental matters or you are the most organized of the whole group or you know how to cook phenomenally.

Trust me, you can turn any of the 4 skills into profitable businesses. So go ahead, ask your friends what they think you're good at and jot down your skills on the list.

Very important!

Don't copy ideas, you'll screw it up quickly. Soon you will have to talk to your customers about the products you sell, give them more details, and teach them how to use them. The point is to understand what you are selling and be 100% convinced that you would buy that product from you.

Don't do everything just for money, show the market that you know how to do things better and I assure you that your efforts will be rewarded.

What do you do Saturday morning?

I usually wake up at 7 o'clock every day, whether it's Saturday or Wednesday.

Now, for me, every morning is an opportunity to solve something related to companies, events, to put the country on track. For you it can mean something completely different: maybe you read (and it's important to write down what you usually read), maybe you watch something, etc.

Think about what you could do all day without getting bored, or if you want, imagine that you are locked in a room with a friend: what topic could you tell them about for 3 hours straight?

At the end of this exercise you should have a list of at least 20 business ideas. If you haven't, go through all the steps again and complete your list. It's important to have a choice, not to wake up during the execution of an idea that it was better if you did something else.

How do you initially estimate the profitability of your idea?

You use a supply and demand matrix, consisting of four alternatives.

First, your business/product idea might command a high price - you have a good profit margin, but few customers. Think of companies like Rolls Royce or Louis Vuitton - they impose a cost that can be borne by a small customer market.

Second, you could ask for a slightly lower price, but target a larger group of customers. Apple, Victoria's Secret - this is the kind of brand with premium products that even the financially middle-class audience can afford.

Third, you could ask for a low price that everyone, the mass of consumers, can afford. Think books like Buyology (I recommend you read it) - they have a wide audience, but a small price.

Lastly, here are the ideas that have both a limited audience and a price per product with a small profit margin. Any product idea that falls into this category is destined to fail.

So, no matter how attached you are to a business idea, if it falls into the last category, give it up immediately. Don't invest resources and feelings in something that is meant to disappoint you from the start.

In principle, your business idea dictates the type of self-products in which you are going to activate, so I will only give you a minimum of advice for choosing them.

Think about the type of consumer you are targeting. In general, it's about those who have a problem, and you offer them the right solution or a better solution than what exists on the market. You can also target enthusiasts, those who would use the products for pleasure, not because they are pressured by some problem.

Then think strictly about your product: what commercial addition can you apply, what is the profit margin, what claims do the producers and suppliers have, what expenses would you end up with the transport company due to the size or weight of the parcels, about what subjects could you write on blog or in company guides related to products.

Other primary characteristics by which to choose the product are its size, the degree of recurrence of purchases (for example, you can count on your fingers the occasions in life when a person buys a refrigerator, but pet food can be purchased even more often than once per month), the possibility of upselling with various accessories, as well as whether the product can be found locally.

TESTING THE MARKET IN A SPECIFIC WAY

Minimum Viable Product - Product prototype

In general, people misunderstand or incompletely understand the idea of MVP. Is it the first version of the product? A validation test? A method to prioritize requirements?

An MVP is the simplest form of your idea that can be sold as a complete product. Comparatively, let's say you want to sell a super futuristic car. Therefore, you can test your idea starting from the sale of a Dacia 1310, a Tesla and then your new car with full functionality.

Now, to build an MVP you establish from the start what the basic functionalities of your product are and then you start aggressively promoting it.

Use a landing page, a blog or the website where you are going to make your store, describe your product / products and invite people to pre-order or leave your email address to be notified when it is launched.

Obviously, you will have to invest a little to drive traffic to that site. A good and fast method is to do a teasing campaign with PPC and optimize the landing page for conversion.

Now that you already have your own stocks, that you do dropshipping, that you make the product from scratch at the time of the order - it's nobody's business. It also matters to the consumer and to maintain the relationship with him after the order. ark and you If you see that people are not interested, if you invest a lot in a campaign or in relevant channels and still don't get the expected results, it's a strong signal for you.

It's a signal that you have to give up the respective products / business idea and reorient yourself, before you lose financially, where it hurts the most.

We are still making developments based on this system. You always have things to add to a digital product, functionalities, requirements and ideas.

This whole process is extremely time-, energy-, and money-consuming, which is why every decision must be well calculated.

You can work day and night for 3 months for a certain application, which in the end works well, looks good and everything is ok, but you see that it doesn't catch on, no one or very few use it. Yes, this has happened to us a few times.

Now we do everything as efficiently as possible. The first step for new developments is up to 80%, the basic version that works, can be used and tested. After we see that everything is ok, based on the feedback received, new improvements are periodically made to the initial version.

Selling via the shop button on your blog

When I started, the technology was not that advanced, at least not in Romania. Today, however, there are so many ways to test selling a product online that it's hard to decide on just one.

A great test method is selling through a shopping button on your blog. Let's say you already have a blog, you might have one too if it's in a specific niche, that's even better.

Naturally, when you talk about a product / service, you can add the purchase option directly from the blog, without taking the user to another site. Without getting muscle fever from so many clicks.

Basically, you choose the desired product from the list of products already uploaded to the platform, select the information you want to display (price, product image, discount if applicable, number of products available in stock, etc.), edit the button so that match the background image (to contrast with it - I don't recommend a specific color, it depends on the background of your blog) and copy it into the content, where you want to place it.

The technical part usually means installing a plugin or a module or a few lines of code. The rest is just the creativity and editing part.

Simple, isn't it? Well, the shopping button only does part of the job. It works and sells, but it matters where you put it. It is important to have a community around the blog, to be relevant in context (you are not trying to sell tires when you write about the latest fashion trends for autumn-winter), as well as the tone of the written articles.

Articles written strictly for sale can be seen and felt. Instead, if you tell people, use natural language and exemplify real situations, then you can sell even on the blog.

Testing on AD websites

We were talking in the previous chapter about classifieds sites (ebay, OLX, Craigslist, etc.). Even if you can't say you have a real business on these sites, you can use them to test sell your products, arrive at a suitable price, and test how you handle product delivery.

I recommend starting here with a price higher than what you want to get, to leave some room for negotiation with your customers. See how much they are willing to pay and that way you will find the right price to sell in your store.

Also, pay close attention to whether and if customers show interest in your type of product. If weeks go by and not even one user asks you for information / order, then it's time to refocus (or try another test method).

Analysis of the opinions and complaints of potential customers

One of the best ways to find out the opinion of customers / Polenqali customers is to ask them personally. My opinion is that the analysis of the messages left by existing customers on competitors or on forums is not conclusive, like the presentation of the prototype or the pre-sale.

However, I recommend that you document yourself from the existing resources, because that's how you shoot a bunch of ducks with a single bullet. On the one hand, it is the consumers' interest in a product similar to the one you are going to sell, you find out what are the dissatisfactions related to the existing solutions (so you can formulate from the start the strengths compared to competing companies), you find out what functionalities or benefits extra want (to build the offer or product / service according to them) and discover where your target audience is.

You can discover more potential customers on Facebook, in a specific group, on a forum, on a blog, etc. Therefore, you can adjust your store implementation and launch strategy to be present on the respective channels.

Start by searching for your product name plus *"opinions"*, *"opinions"*, *"reviews"* or even phrases with *"what do you think about"*, *"advantages"*, *"disadvantages"*, etc. Enter as many sources as possible and write down your essentials. You can also search for various Facebook groups related to your product or its features.

For example, maybe you want to sell baby car seats - in which case I doubt you'll find a dedicated group just for that, but you can head over to mums and dads groups and look for discussions or even ask questions.

NPS - Net Promoter Score

Recently we had such an action in the company and we chose to do it by phone. Basically, our support team called all customers paying the form to see and better understand the degree of satisfaction or dissatisfaction. What I want to mention here is that regardless of the grade given, we also asked the reason, to see what and where it needs to be improved. I learned a lot from this action: communication must always be improved between the supplier and the customer, different customer segments give different answers, and the WOW effect only happens once.

How likely are you to recommend us to a friend or acquaintance? This is the question you ask when you want to find out your NPS, using a scale of 0 to 10.

The answers fall into 3 fractions:
- **Promoters** (grade 9-10) are the loyal customers and followers who not only buy, but also tell others about your company.
- **Passives** (grade 7-8) are ok, but not so impressed by your brand, so they can easily buy from the competition, without thinking too much.
- **Detractors** (grade (-6) are dissatisfied customers, for reasons or not, but you have to be very careful about them because they can tarnish your reputation and image by speaking publicly about their dissatisfaction

How do you calculate NPS? Using the formula NPS = Promoters - Detractors. Your score can go from -100 - if everyone is dissatisfied, to 100 - if everyone is a promoter and brand ambassador.

How do you improve your NPS? You will learn everything in this book, especially the chapter dedicated to customer loyalty.

Talk to people

Also on the idea of questions, create a questionnaire (there are a lot of tools, you can also use Google Forms) and share it on social networks or place it in the landing page of the presentation of the product prototype. You can display it here when people express their intention to leave the site - you ask them what products they would be interested in, why they chose to leave without leaving your contact details or pre-ordering.

Or you can display it in a pop-up when they enter the site and offer them a discount / other type of benefit for answering your questions.

Another way to find out the opinions and complaints of potential customers is to carefully analyze the websites and social media pages of competing companies in the market where you want to sell.

Look at reviews, testimonials, ratings, discussions, comments, etc. and learn indirectly, also from consumers, what to do or what to avoid in presenting and selling your products. Take the time and inclination to also watch the comments on YouTube videos about the products in question.

You can also do this at large stores in the country or abroad, for the type of product you sell.

Following trends with Google Trends

One thing we haven't discussed so far is seasonality - of products, implicitly of business ideas. There are types of products that sell better at one time of the year, and the rest of the time have sporadic sales or even none at all

Why? Look, think about fashion, pool cleaning services, building materials, power plants, flooring or even stationery. You don't sell the same collection of clothes in summer as you do in winter. You sell paper products all year round, but you have a fantastic boom near the start of the school year or during a school year. Or you will have a few customers throughout the year if you sell wedding invitations with steady sales and even peaks between May and September.

Seasonality represents peaks and troughs in interest for certain products or services, influenced by external elements: weather, events. ments, seasons, habits, political, climatic, financial changes, etc.

Seasonality, among other factors, determines what we call trends - fluctuations in consumer behavior and purchasing patterns. Some products are bought all year round (eg bread), others are consumed at specific times (eg watermelons or ice cream or fridges on Black Friday).

Now, in order to test your business idea and the salability of the products, it is necessary to take these trends into account, specifically for your case.

Google provides you with a free tool to identify trends in your sector. They are displayed to you based on the searches made by users, at the level of country, location, similar keywords, similar topics, on a time interval that you set yourself. Google Trends even shows you YouTube searches.

Search for trends for your products using various keywords, including longer phrases, and see what the user interest graph is. Obviously, Google Trends isn't the only tool you can use. Look for market studies in your niche - they also show you details and details that you can't find with Trends.

Facebook Shop

The last testing method I'll talk about in more detail here is the Facebook store. And you are probably now thinking why we didn't introduce this option to the business types in the previous chapter.

Simple, the Facebook store is not for everyone and comes with a series of advantages and disadvantages or risks, so to speak.

In principle, Facebook or any other social network is not intended for sale from the start. Usually, people come in to post, chat with friends, and socialize. The organic posts of a business page are very different from the posts of friends and, more than that, on Facebook the potential

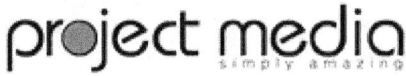

customer does not come prepared with his wallet or card, with the intention of buying something.

The Facebook store is good for creating brand recognition from the target audience and for testing these recognition elements (logo, slogan, product images, approach, etc.). It's also a good start to building a community around your brand, which you can then draw into the site - where the sale happens.

Facebook gives you the option of adding a new tab to your page for creating a store - and how to do this exactly can be found in the network's support service.

The best thing about this testing method is that you don't need a domain. Until you solve the details such as domain, hosting, design, etc., you can test and even sell with the help of the Facebook store.

FINDING & EVALUATING COMPETITION

In my field (implicitly yours, since you want your own business) there is a saying: good marketers spend a lot of time analyzing the competition. Exceptional marketers spend even more time analyzing the competition.

However, I'm not telling you to become more obsessed with the competition than with your own store. Yes, it is important to keep an eye on these "c's", but there is no need to analyze them daily, obsessively, ignoring what is happening in your garden. You can like their Facebook page or subscribe to their newsletter to see communications, that's enough for a start.

Remember how I compared today's market to an ocean full of sharks? Well, buckle up, you're about to become a shark too. And in order to reach your target audience, you need to know what other competitors are doing, how they manage to attract customers and convince them to buy.

Want more reasons why competitive analysis is necessary? First of all, this is how you find the strengths and weaknesses of these companies. By following the strong points, you realize which functionalities or benefits you will struggle with, and by following the weak points, you realize what you have to do to cover them in your product or store.

Second, I doubt there is any serious store owner out there who set out to do exactly what the competition is doing or want to run the same kind of campaigns and promotions.

Nobody enters a business because they want to be the same as competing companies. On the contrary, he wants to do at least something different. Therefore, you need to know what your competition is doing, in order not to become a copy of it.

Now that you understand why it's important to track your competitors, it's time to find out how to do it. And here you will need to understand the concept of keywords in search engines.

Basically, use the name of the product types you want to sell and search for them on Google. See who the returned results are from on the first page or even further if you want. Go to those sites and write down their names along with the key terms you used.

One more thing, you may already have some competitors in mind. I don't know, maybe it's a small store with which you're sure you're competing in terms of turnover. Online, however, you are in direct competition with the sites that are displayed higher on the front page with the results returned when you search for the keywords you want to use.

How is the actual analysis done? Once you have identified your competitors, create a table (you can use Excel) and write down:

- what products/services do they sell;
- what is the authority and seniority of each competitor (you can use archive.org/web);
- what are the strategies addressed in the past versus the strategies addressed currently;
- what type of media channels they use to promote their products;
- an estimate of the resources invested in promotion;
- what is the type of assistance provided to customers, as well as its quality;
- brand mentions;
- the type of content published;
- site loading speed;
- the keywords they are well positioned on.

Then head over to their Social Media pages and find out what type of content they're promoting, how often and when they're posting, what products their competitors' customers like the most, what their fan reactions and reviews are, what they're promoting through paid ads, and what types of ads i use

You can also subscribe to competing sites to find out what emails they send, what they look like, what products they promote, when they send them and how often.

In addition to all these manual actions you do, you can use competitor analysis tools, such as SimilarWeb, CognitiveSEO, BuzzSumo, etc. Some of these even allow you to set alerts to receive periodic reports or warnings. That way you can focus on your online store, without feeling the need to obsessively spy on your competitors.

We have already established that you need to do a competitive analysis of this first phase, when you have just finished building your demand plan and are about to launch your business. The analysis of the competitor is constantly, somehow continuously, but with the instrumental help that I mentioned before, when a new competitor appears on the market and when the existing competitors launch a new product / service on the market.

Any small detail that you have in addition / better than the competition can make the difference.

Therefore, look for weaknesses in the competition. There you will find the means by which to do things differently, smarter, and thus get not only more sales, but also more satisfied customers, who will continue to talk about you.

LEGAL ASPECTS RELATED TO YOUR ONLINE BUSINESS

The privacy policy is a vital element because this is how you explain to the user why you collect his personal data and how you process it, including the free movement of data.

Even more so today, the privacy policy is no longer a fad, thanks to the GDPR. This is where you need to tell people what data you collect, why, how long it stays in your possession, who has access to it, and inform them of their rights over the data you hold. Make sure you have a link to this page throughout your site and next to the consent request boxes under any form.

In the same way, it is necessary to display the information policy for cookies and not to send promotional messages to people who have not given your consent.

GDPR in a nutshell

GDPR is a new regulation of the European Union that increases the level of protection of personal data of EU residents.

In other words, it imposes certain obligations on organizations that process this type of data, whether online or offline. Including you.

Your online store can collect data following orders (name, surname, address, social security number, contact data such as email address or phone number, biometric data or images), visitor data on web pages (IP address, placement of cookies), newsletter subscription data, employee data, data from job candidate CVs, etc.

According to the GDPR, any process of processing confidential data must have a clear basis, and the people who provide you with this data must give you clear and explicit consent. For example, data may be collected to:

- concluding or executing a contract (such as processing an order and delivering products);
- because the person in question has given you consent (for example, to be targeted with marketing campaigns);
- achieving the legitimate interests pursued by you as an operator or by a third party;
- fulfilling a legal obligation that falls to you;
- fulfilment of a task that serves a vested interest resulting from the exercise of the public authority announced by the operator;
- protecting the vital interests of the person concerned or another natural person.

Any visitor to the website must be informed in a common and easy-to-understand language about why you want to process their data, but also about their rights. You are also responsible for the collected data, and in the event of a breach, you notify the Authority within 72 hours at most.

Consumer rights are now extended to include the following:

- the right to information - the person can ask you what you want to do with his data;
- the right to access data - he can ask you to see how, for what purpose his data is processed and who has access to it; the right to rectification - may ask you to correct or complete the data;
- the right to delete data - applies under certain conditions. For example, if he asks you for this as soon as he has completed an order, you still have to keep his data until you honor the contract, and then delete them;
- the right to restrict processing;
- the right to data portability;
- the right to opposition;
- the right not to be subject to an automatic individual decision;
- the right to address the Website Authority.

Although a few months / days before the application of the GDPR, many were struggling to solve only the technical part for obtaining consent (collection of emails and cookies), the idea is that you must also have a well-established internal organization. And I strongly believe that many have forgotten - still - about it.

Internally you need protocols for securing access to data, appointing a data protection officer, a data protection and retention policy, a problem intervention and notification process, and a secure transfer procedure from one operator to another. another.

On a technical level, most platforms have come with specific modules for GDPR.

The GDPR did nothing more than ensure the implementation of previous data protection rules by threatening higher fines and giving extended rights to consumers. Which, from my point of view, is perfectly normal.

If until now you thought that the new regulation is an obstacle to your business, my advice is to get rid of the worry. As long as you do things correctly, carefully and transparently, you are safe.

TECHNICAL ASPECTS RELATED TO YOUR ONLINE BUSINESS. HOW TO CHOOSE THE E-COMMERCE PLATFORM

There is no one best eCommerce platform that is perfect for everyone and works masterfully for any type of online business. So keep this fact firmly in mind.

On the other hand, there is the best eCommerce platform for you and your needs. After this kind of technical magic you should be focusing on. And one more thing, there are no free eCommerce platforms. It is simply impossible to create an online store for free. Think about everything you need to get it up and running: domain, hosting, SSL certificates, maintenance and custom mods or modules if applicable. All of this costs money.

Depending on the platform you choose, these costs may be higher or lower, but never, absolutely never, free.

I feel like I need to push this thing with the costs of an eCommerce platform a bit because most of the questions on profile / web groups revolve around looking for a free platform.

Why should you look beyond cost when choosing an eCommerce platform? Because, basically, it's a fundamental solution for the function and even the existence of your store, and it's ridiculous to condition it on such a misleading factor as the price.

Imagine you've found the perfect platform, it's free and...um, that's about it. You don't know how to configure the products, you have limited design options such that your store is one and the same as the other thousand other stores present on the platform (or if you want a different theme, take the money out of your wallet and the freebie goes away), you have no security , maybe you don't have support, it's not scalable and so on.

What are you doing? If you don't know what to do, you pay others to do it for you. Or even if you have technical knowledge, tell me what you want to be: programmer or online store owner? Do you think you'll have time to be both at once?

The free eCommerce platform is a bigger paradox than the crocodile paradox, with which the world's greatest philosophers have been scratching their heads for centuries. Now and once and for all, the definition of

the right eCommerce platform is this: the best eCommerce platform is the one that fits your current needs, but can also adapt in the future, should you want to expand.

There is a partial misconception in the eCommerce market that you can start with one platform and then change it over and over whenever you want or you're not satisfied. But those who have done at least one migration from one platform to another know that the job is not as simple as it seems, not to mention the serious problems that arise from a faulty migration. Oh, or the migration costs and the data you might lose.

Yes, if you made the wrong choice, it's normal to migrate, to want to change the platform, but that's exactly why you're reading the book, to find out how to make the best decision for you from the start.

Look for answers

Is the platform multi-channel? How can I explain it to you, today you only sell and survive in the market if you are present on the channels where your customers are also. In other words, it is not enough to just have a website and wait for customers to start ordering. You have to go to all the channels that bring you sales: on Social Media, marketplace, to affiliates, on price comparators and so on.

The desired platform allows you easy integrations with these third parties and you have to request the development team of additional modules, just for you.

Does the platform grow with the business? Is it scalable? Look at the maximum number of products you can sell on that platform (whether it's a SaaS, look at the other subscriptions, not just the one you can afford now).

Each platform has certain limits related to the maximum number of users, products, hardware specifications, etc. Or, please, these limits are imposed by the cost you are willing to accept.

It also tracks the sites in the platform portfolio, with a larger number of products, and sees how they move, how the site loads, and what additional features it has. Analyzing these sites you realize for real how scalable the platform is.

Further, track how secure your store is on the platform. Any solution operates with personal data, and it must be stored on secure servers, monitored 24/7, otherwise problems arise and your business reputation is compromised (not to mention fines). In this case, customers no longer have the confidence to buy, and without customers, you have no sales. Without sales, you can close your business and the dream is over.

So, look for a well-secured platform and pay attention to SSL certificates, who implements them for your site (preferably the developer team behind the platform).

Then, pay attention to the location of the platform, an aspect closely related to the support part. If you want to sell internationally or in Europe, you can use either a domestic or an international platform.

Does the platform provide you with integrations with other systems? And with what systems? To function correctly and for promotion, you need additional integrations with: courier companies, payment processors, Google Analytics, product analyzers, ERP (if applicable), management, invoicing, email marketing systems, marketing automation, etc. Are there already pre-integrations for the analyzed platform or do you need to ask for the development of additional modules? What are the costs?

It is also important that the platform ensures you integrate future systems (don't forget, technology is developing day by day). How do you figure out how the platform moves over time? Follow the chats of current customers, and see the pace at which updates and modules are made in the platform. Is this constantly evolving? It means that they will adapt to everything new in the market, before you ask the team.

Does the platform in question have all the modules and functionalities you need for the specifics of your store? Online sales is a pretty complicated business anyway so you need to make sure you have powerful tools to deal with the needs of the public and the threats of the competition.

First of all, you need modules for managing your store: adding products, including import / export, advanced product configuration, order management, including phone orders, theme editing, creating and editing pages, customer management, reports and so on.

Secondly, you need modules that determine conversions: various types and discount rules, vouchers, creation of landing pages, hello bar, forms, etc. Then follow the marketing functions that the platform offers you, natively. You see, nowadays, marketing modules are 100% mandatory for an eCommerce platform, otherwise it's as if they convey to the user that they can sell without promoting themselves. Which is totally false. See if the platform is ready for SEO, email marketing, customer loyalty, abandoned cart recovery, integrations with PPC tools.

Another aspect to consider when choosing a platform is support. Do you have support by email, phone, tickets, etc., from a well-trained team? Can you get along with the people behind the platform or do you speak different languages, both literally and figuratively? Do you have documentation, a help center so you can manage your store and admin panel?

Last but not least, see if the platform really helps you sell; You have complete ways of marketing the product, cross-sell, unsell, bundle, associating products with different types of blog content, etc.

Now, if you have something more advanced in mind, choose a platform that also has the ability to run multiple sites on a single infrastructure, allows you to launch with new brands and in other countries or with other business models (marketplace, dropshipping, etc.) and providing support for different buying behaviors and levels of authority management.

I know, I have listed many features here, but I assure you that there are not one, but several platforms available on the market that meet the conditions. But above these, the most important factor for choosing an eCommerce platform is trust.

It is vital to constantly and actively interact with the people behind the platform (agency, developer, developer team), every time it is needed. If you don't know how to do something or need help, it's perfectly normal to ask them directly, be transparent and have a civil conversation.

You also need to understand that you have your rights and responsibilities, as well as theirs. Nobody is nobody's slave, and things can be resolved politely.

Think of your relationship with the platform as a marriage. For things to work, trust, communication and understanding are needed on both sides. Mistakes happen all the time, no one makes mistakes on purpose.

The team behind the platform must understand when you need help, even for tasks that seem simple to them. On the other hand, you must understand that a platform means the hard work of some people who have to live in turn and get paid.

Because if you don't handle things with trust and communication, you end up with divorce. And, just like in a marriage, it is expensive, problematic and causes loss on both sides.

Types of eCommerce platforms

Now that we've discussed the criteria for choosing an eCommerce platform that's right for you, it's time to find out what types of platforms are available to you.

First, we have the open-source platforms, those that are partially free or wrongly perceived as free.

The attraction to open-source platforms is mainly motivated by the sense of ownership of the online store, as well as access to the code. Technical knowledge is mandatory if you choose such a platform - or, alternatively, you agree with a programmer or a specialized agency to handle these tasks.

Honestly, I think that these types of platforms are more suitable for developers, not for you - the end customer, because logically, an entrepreneur should be oriented towards business, not towards programming. When you want to sell and grow a business, believe me you don't even have 24 hours in a day, let alone learn and schedule.

Compared to other platforms, the costs for open-source are related to hosting, the initial setup of the store, the design and theme of the site, as well as the costs of buying modules, plus modifying them, often being adapted only for the international market .

Second, we have the SaaS / rented / paid monthly or yearly platforms. Somehow, this type of platform is the exact opposite of open-source platforms. Here you don't need technical knowledge because the code part is stored in the cloud and accessed only by the team that provides you with this solution. The rented platform comes with a hosting assistant included for the store, as well as a guarantee for any technical or security problems.

SaaS platforms are suitable for most types of online businesses because they offer different subscriptions, depending on the number of items sold, but also on the specific needs of businesses.

As for the costs, it's about the subscription itself, additional developments, maintenance and, depending on which solution you choose, the platform can ask for a commission from your sales.

Thirdly, there are the custom platforms. The truth is that even the big brands in the market no longer choose such a platform. It involves a horribly large, and ultimately unnecessary, investment. Rather, they look to what already exists in the market and hire teams to make the desired developments in the initial infrastructure.

Now you know how to choose the platform. Apply the question matrix to the solutions you have in mind and see which can answer all your questions and needs. Then test - most platforms offer you a free trial period to find out for yourself whether or not they really match what you're looking for.

Choosing the hosting / domain name

At this stage, we implicitly discuss the name of your company, which we have been putting off until now. Why? Because the domain name should be related to the company name.

Ultimate eCommerce Masterplan - Nistor Zsolt

project media

When you choose the company name / domain name, try to find a short name, easy to pronounce, remember and write (be careful with the name in English, everyone pronounces it the way they like), a name that summarizes the essence of your brand or to describe it, try to avoid using numbers or hyphens and think long-term - a renaming process takes time, is expensive and causes quite a lot of loss.

You can use name generators, you can come up with new, original names or word combinations - whichever method you use, check that they are not registered trademarks and, ideally, that they are available as domain names.

Oh, and one more thing. Avoid domain names made up of exact keywords. eveningdresses.com, housewindows2018.com, funnypartyhats.com - all these exact keywords can bury you in Google. Yes, there was a time when exact keyword domains gave you maximum SEO visibility, but now they can give you penalties and drops in visibility.

As for the domain extension (.ro, .com, .net, etc.), choose according to the market you intend to target. Do you want to sell wheels? Choose a .ro domain and hosting from Romania - besides the fact that the site will load faster, and Google takes into account the place where you are hosted, favoring the site in searches on google.ro. Instead, if you want to sell globally or in Europe, choose the .com extension and hosting from Romania or other countries.

Next, how do you choose hosting for your website? I'll start by mentioning that SaaS platforms provide you with hosting for files, images, etc., but hosting and domain are separate and up to you.

For the choice of hosting you will have to take into account several important factors because you certainly do not want to wake up with your eyes in the sun and the site down when the world is most dear to you (such as on Black Friday or in the middle of a campaign of marketing that you worked hard on).

What are these factors?

First of all, if you want to sell in your country, choose a hosting provider from your country - in addition to the higher loading speed, you quickly find the relevant people when a problem arises. You have to be extremely lucky to never have a problem. They inevitably occur, but it would be best if they occur because of you, and the hosting people help you bring things back to normal.

I do not recommend that you go to providers that promise you unlimited hosting, with unlimited traffic, for free. You know how it is, when everything sounds too good to be true, something is fishy in the middle. Check the uptime (the time the site is up and perfectly accessible) in general, talk to people who already have sites hosted by the provider you are interested in, see how they manage the relationship with them and the problems.

Also, see how the hosting provider stands in terms of security.

BEAUTY IS IN THE EYES OF THE BEHOLDER - WEB DESIGN

If, once you've reached this step, you're expecting me to give you the perfect recipe for web design, I'm afraid I'm going to disappoint you. As in the flat case in the form of eCommerce, there is no fixed and best thing; we also take into account the fact that trends change from year to year.

The big problem in web design is the discrepancy between what your client wants and what you want to do. You see, you can't go to the developer or the team you work with and say *"I want a site like eMAG"* or *"I want to use white, red, green and orange, keep it minimalistic"* or *"I want a red background , but I also want the buttons to be red, because I heard they attract the most clicks"*. Web design goes hand in hand with the concept of usability, the degree of ease with which the customer navigates and navigates your site.

So you can go to the developer and ask for anything you can think of, but you'll have a site that you or your friends or family like, and that's it. Customers will not be able to handle it and will have problems ordering, therefore they will probably go to the competition.

The first and most important rule of thumb when it comes to your website design is about focusing on the user/customer experience.

But what makes for a good user experience? In the world of web design, we have two separate but equally important concepts: UI - user interface (represents the totality of aspects with which the user interacts when navigating the site; the elements that the user will use) and UX - user experience (the totality of things from the site that lead to a good experience; what the user feels when using the site).

An example from practice: UI is the internal search box positioned at the top of the screen, and UX is the feeling of clarity and ease in finding the desired product. Or UI is the use of different font sizes in strategic places on the web page, and UX is the ease with which the user can scan the page and discover / understand the information they are looking for.

A good web designer knows how to combine these two concepts to give you a design that helps you sell - ultimately, the purpose for which you are building your online store.

You can't just throw different elements into every store web page and expect to be successful. You need a clear information architecture. And the customization part takes even more time and effort, which is why web design costs.

For the design of your website, start from the idea that no one knows who you are, what you do and what you sell. Remember that you have a maximum of 5 seconds from the moment of access to impress the user, otherwise he leaves.

And with mobile users, you have an even shorter time to make a good first impression. Therefore, the visuals and text on any store page must be obvious, explicit, crystal clear or whatever synonym you want to use.

Today, a good layout for an online store is a modern site with a clean design. Avoid cluttering the background, using a rainbow of colors and varieties of fonts, especially if they are not supported by the browser.

Also, your website design should highlight your business's unique value proposition through a clear message, large and quality images, evidence of credibility, and the way information is organized.

Most of the time you can go with confidence on the idea of themes, if you have preset designs for different niches. These themes are thought out, flat and optimized to give your customers the best possible experience and above all for you to have a high conversion rate.

The sin of the newbie entrepreneur comes quickly in the way that many want design elements for their own ego and provide the browsing experience and help conversion.

The problem is that many analyze the graphic elements, even the commerce, from a large screen of a laptop or PC, ask for certain graphic "loads" of design and forget that most users arrive in the store and buy from a mobile device, which they are not displaying the same elements.

Also, these graphics can significantly increase a page's load time, which leads to decreased sales.

When you want to have something unique in this regard, ask the opinion of an expert and see how to find a middle ground that reconciles your ideas with good UX practices.

Today, the cool part is that you can test the impact of certain graphics on sales. I recommend that you make decisions based on data, more than on the basis of "this is how I feel, this is what I want".

Creating an eye-catching logo

This works like the suit you wear for an interview with a potential employer. It makes a first impression and conveys a few essential things about yourself.

You, future store owner, are aware that you need a logo, an identity system that will take you out into the world, introduce you to customers. But in most cases, many put off creating these visuals because of the cost.

Obviously, if you have some knowledge in the field you can create your own logo. But in my experience, most platform or web design clients prefer to use our graphic designer for logo creation.

Based on his work and best practices in the market, your store logo should be simple and easy to understand (no fillers, unnecessary elements) and, above all, fit your business, make sense for customers. You should also make the logo timeless, think of it for future goals as well. For example, if you want to start with a jewelry catalog and then expand to cosmetics or bookstores, it is not advisable to have a logo that includes a pair of earrings, no matter how stylized they are.

Additionally, you can go for a brightly colored logo, but that doesn't mean that black and white logos have a lower impact. If it is colored, make sure that the logo is recognizable even if it is printed in black and white on promotional products, parcels, letterheads, etc.

Finally, don't forget, both the logo and the theme and design of your store must align with your unique value proposition, convey a unified message - the essence of your brand.

BRIEF GUIDE TO STOCK & DELIVERY

Inventory management for your online store

Well, this is where the madness begins. Inventory control is the worst part of the business, robbing even the most experienced store owners of sleep. If by now you've read a lot about online commerce and how easy it is to open such a business, it's time to enter the even less glossy part of the process of creating your business.

It's easy to get carried away by reading about usability, marketing and other things, but to see the hassle when you receive the long-awaited order and you don't have the product in stock or at the supplier, to deliver it to the customer. For this reason, it is vital that you now organize the most suitable form of stock for you, as well as its management.

The truth is that over 60% of online stores work with supplier stocks. It's perfectly legal and a less risky form of stock, especially if you're just starting out and can't afford to invest in your own stock and all that comes with it (storage, staff, insurance, etc.).

Now, there are situations, and different ways of approaching stocks for each situation.

Own stock

Let's say that maybe you're the maker of the products you sell - maybe you have a business in the handmade niche. In this case, your inventory represents current assets in production and in the form of raw materials for manufacturing products, materials and other consumables (such as packaging).

In the beginning, you can anticipate a higher demand for top products and / or produce a minimum number of products required for each category you intend to sell. Thus, the moment you launch your store and the orders arrive, you can deliver them immediately.

For the rest of the products, you need to maintain a stock of raw materials so that you can start manufacturing immediately and minimize the lead time as much as possible. When the number of orders is low and the business is small, you can afford to keep the stocks at home or in the garage and keep track of them in a spreadsheet.

MANAGING STOCKS

But, as the business grows, implicitly the number of orders, this form of stock is no longer profitable. You will definitely need to hire staff, rent / buy a work space and manage stocks with the help of automations.

On the other hand, if you sell products from suppliers, you have more possibilities at your disposal. If you have the resources for a serious investment in stocks, you could work with your own stocks.

What are the advantages here? In principle, you can deliver the products faster, have a higher conversion rate and a lower number of cancellations / returns.

But the own stocks also come with a series of problems for the blocked capital, for the products themselves, the cost of storing them in the right conditions, the cost of protecting the products (from fires, natural disasters, etc.), the cost of handling their products (employees and management programs, packaging, etc.), the need to understand the importance of stock rotation and its speed, but also the problem of finding products in the warehouse.

If you want and can work with your own stocks, you either create your own logistics flow (from storage, stock handling, packaging and delivery), or you outsource to an e-fulfillment service (Frisbo, Fulfill. ro, etc.) and things are simplified a lot.

In the event that you work personally with your own stocks, I recommend you to orient yourself towards the profile materials and sites because the strategy is quite long and complex.

Stocks at the supplier

The second situation is the sale without stock or with stock at the supplier. Basically, you don't have to worry about storage space or money stuck in stock, you only buy the product when the customer orders it.

Obviously, the store without stock is not only milk and honey, but also a set of risks that you take. You have higher costs when buying products because you don't buy them in bulk, you have to synchronize your stock information with the supplier's, and there is a possibility that one or more products may be out of stock after you receive an order. During peak periods such as Black Friday or other seasonal / discount campaigns, all these issues become even more pressing.

If you order from the supplier, the product comes to you and you take care of its packaging and delivery, there is also the problem of extended deadlines. But today, most product suppliers are willing to handle the packaging, invoicing and delivery of the product directly to the customer on your behalf.

Since each of the situations presented comes with disadvantages, you could turn to a middle solution: to have your own stock with the top best-selling products (what you predict will sell more) and to order the rest from the supplier. I'm not going to mention now how mandatory own stocks are when you get to enterprise level, because that's another topic, for another book.

Whatever your situation, you need to estimate your inventory cost based on which product lines you plan to stock, how many of each product line you'll need to open the store, and what your recommended cost is. supplier for each of these products.

Also, make a realistic strategy about your stocks: talk to various suppliers and find out if they are open to a collaboration of the type you want, enter into well-established contracts and fight to be treated as a priority, even if you are beginning and maybe you don't have experience.

Regarding stock management, at a low volume of stocks and products, let's say it is possible to do it manually, but my recommendation is to choose an automatic management program. There are options on the market (SmartBill, ERP programs, own applications from the eCommerce platform, etc.).

Using these types of tools, you also get rid of the problem of invoices / receipts, and reports on transactions in your online store.

Also, request a product file from suppliers to make a product list and integrate your suppliers in the platform to have the stock situation up to date, permanently.

The delivery strategy of your online store

Your store's delivery strategy has long ceased to mean just moving the product from point A to point B. It depends both on the operation of the business, customer satisfaction and platform on the brand. What do I mean?

Chances are you've had at least one bad experience too, or if that's not enough googling. There are hundreds of comments and horror stories about the experience with couriers, and the saddest thing is that the dissatisfaction also spills over to online stores that collaborate with companies that, apparently, have a little worse organization than a football team in the fifth league.

At this moment, when you have to choose the delivery strategy and the partners you will work with, you have to take into account what I have been telling you in the book. I insist on this because, as with the platform, hosting or design, many people run after the lowest price.

The delivery strategy of your online store depends on a set of business-specific factors. Not every shipping method or courier company is right for everyone (similar to the platform, remember?).

Before you start looking for partners, take a moment and think about your brand, where products come from, where they need to go, average order value, product weight, profit margin, tracking and insurance preferences parcels, customer preferences, but also the rules of courier companies, the cost of products, rules and restrictions related to products, as well as customization possibilities

Sort each factor separately in a list / table and sketch table and sketch a first template of the delivery strategy. You see, sometimes I can't afford or from the point of view of cost to send a product with a shipping company. For example, it would be ridiculous to want to send a fridge to a customer with a bicycle courier. On the other hand, you have other costs if the package has to reach a more remote place and the courier has to cover additional kilometers.

Also related to costs, you have to think carefully about how much it costs the customer to get possession of his order. According to the latest statistics, Romanians love online stores that offer free shipping, and run away from companies that unpleasantly surprised them with unexpected prices, boom... on the order completion page.

Obviously, you don't have to say OK, I'm just offering free shipping and I'll have sky-high sales (but with a below-sea-level profit). There are many things you can do, starting with total honesty with your customer on your product pages. You can recommend the customer to choose the desired product variant, and then you automatically show him the shipping price. Or you can impose an amount for the value of the basket, above which he can enjoy free delivery.

Whatever you choose, be completely transparent with the customer and don't hide the real costs from them until the last minute. Even if he makes the purchase on impulse, he will think twice when he sees additional shipping costs on the checkout page.

Who do you deliver with?

Well, now that we've established that, once again, the customer dictates, it's time to think about the practical mode of transportation you'll implement. And here, you have more options.

First of all, you can allow customers to pick up products from the office. sir, it seems to me a good method for orders from the same city, especially if you are the manufacturer of the products or have them in stock. Thus you could fill ridiculously long waiting times if the customer is sitting right next to you or is willing to make a trip to your premises.

If you offer customers the opportunity to interact with you or your employees at the headquarters, don't forget that you also need a cash register. In the same idea, locally you could implement your own delivery system, with the company car. I don't jump at the idea of a fleet of cars, because I'm aware, most small business owners don't have enough funds for such a thing from the start.

For example, if you sell custom t-shirts or any other product, you could offer the customer the opportunity to receive the product at their home, office or mutually agreed upon location, directly from you / your employee. Believe me, customers see this option as a favor, they are not so demanding that they will not accept anything other than delivery by courier, directly to the door.

In this situation, if you see that the person is willing, you can chat a little, you can ask him for feedback, you can make a joke and, look, you have more chances to keep him loyal.

If these variants are suitable for the local transport area, we now move on to heavy artillery. When you sell nationally or even abroad, you have the option of working with courier companies (preferred by the majority) or with the Post Office.

In the case of B, using the Post Office, you can use the services intended for online commerce, to avoid long delivery times and the usual problems with standard delivery. Deliveries by Post are preferred by many for orders from rural areas.

Now, about the collaboration with courier companies.

My recommendation is to consider all the courier companies that fit the outline of the delivery strategy (that you made at the beginning). Join the profile groups on Facebook and on the net and see the discussions of other entrepreneurs who are already experienced.

Then contact the courier companies of your choice and discuss the following aspects: package sizes, weight (others are costs for white, large products and others, for small products), shipping and destination country/city, package tracking options , insurance options in case of theft, damage, loss, order volume, your profit margin, parcel delivery and discounts.

You will see that, being at the beginning, it is possible that you will not be noticed by the big companies, especially if you do not have figures related to the volume of orders. That's the reality, it's better to expect from the start, not to be taken by surprise.

Talk to several courier companies and negotiate some prices in the future, you will be able to renegotiate them, depending on how things evolve). Don't necessarily run after the lowest price, but focus on quality and performance. Look for opinions of current customers or, better yet, do some tests. Order from online stores that you know have a contract with the desired courier company and observe the delivery times, the courier's approach, insurance and monitoring systems, etc.

Once you have chosen a company (or several, depending on the factors discussed), enter into contracts with them. The contract brings you advantages such as lower fees for a larger volume and other benefits.

One more thing, see what integration possibilities with courier companies you have in the eCommerce platform and what their costs are.

Product packaging and unpacker experience

Before you think about personalization, you need to address the functional side: you want your products to reach the customer in the best condition, protected from the inevitable effects of transport, such as arranging in the car, dust or others.

Therefore, you must first find the right packaging. Probably the 200-liter cleaning bags are cheaper for you, but keep in mind that the customer experience will be just as cheap / impoverished.

Basically, the package, the packaging used, is the first thing the customer sees and touches. If the excitement of shopping is reduced to a certain extent with online orders (because the person cannot touch the product or see it physically or turn it over on all sides), it must be stimulated at the time of receiving the package.

Now, custom packaging is not a necessity, especially if funds and time are reduced. However, my advice is to adopt a little personalization method as it is one of the cheapest forms of marketing, plus it can make the difference between a customer who comes back to buy and one you never hear from again.

Most online stores are oriented towards a middle way, choosing customization for seasonal purchases, special campaigns or when they receive feedback related to customer preferences.

Regarding standard packaging, I recommend that you stock up on packaging suitable for the dimensions and needs of each product. Obviously you'll want something as compact as possible to keep shipping costs down - I'm thinking you won't be using a cardboard box as much as a microwave for a pair of earrings. For a minimum of personalization, you can use scotch tape with the logo / name of the store and add a thank you note to the package.

Custom packaging

But let's discuss in more detail about the elements you can include in the packaging to make the customer as pleasant a surprise as possible, but also to promote yourself to him.

First, the box, envelope or other. These are actually the first things the customer sees. Here you can play with the shape, the size, the colors, the printed design or any other attributes, in order to emphasize the colors, convey the essence of the brand.

Secondly, pay attention to the protective materials you use; bubble sheets, polystyrene, foam inserts, air cushions, crumpled paper of various colors or any other type of material, in accordance with the needs of the packaged product.

Thirdly, you can use tissue paper in the boxes for an added mystery or to induce a certain mood in the customer, at the time of unpacking. You can customize it with brand insignia, and in seasonal campaigns, you can adjust these insignia to specific symbols for Christmas / Winter, Valentine's Day, Black Friday, Easter, etc.

Then, it's standard to insert the invoice into the package, but you can work on how to present it. Do you think the first thing the customer wants to see when opening is the invoice? I do not think so. You can place it somewhere below, under the product / products or you can insert it in a personalized envelope. Or, even better, email him the invoice. Let the customer enjoy first, don't remind them of the pain of paying first.

Other elements that you can use are personalized scotch, brand insignia, stickers (glued on the box or inserted in the package to be placed on the fridge, laptop, bicycle, etc.), personalized thank you notes, vouchers, product samples extras, small gifts, coupons, invitations to social media or website feedback, hashtag suggestions and so on.

I think by now you have a lot of possible customization ideas in your mind, but I want to draw your attention to one thing. Always take into account the rules of the courier / transport company you work with, each has different rules regarding packaging. Also, if you sell products with stock to the supplier and he takes care of the packaging, make your materials available to him for this process.

Finally, don't forget: the customer experience is the most important. Choose your delivery method, partners and packaging method strategically so that the experience elevates you to the top of stores, not burying you in Google and negative reviews on social media.

CHOICE OF PAYMENT METHODS / PROCESSORS

So we haven't talked about the right price for your products yet?

Since we're talking about payment methods, it's time to remind you of some good practices related to pricing.

Imagine you've found the perfect jacket. It looks fantastic, exactly the model you've been looking for for so long, it feels like it was made just for you... and then you look at the price. You widen your eyes and remain shocked long after you leave the store. Is it made of dragon skin and unicorn tears?! This behavior is typical for brick-and-mortar stores, but price is an equally strong decision-making factor online. Especially since here you don't have to turn the screen to see the price, I notice it from the first, next to the product image (or so it should be).

There are different methods of calculating the price, all depending on some factors that you have to establish in the blood. These are competition, costs and consumer needs. And, be careful, you have to do all of them for the calculation.

I'll start by talking about the competition, although my advice is not to try to beat competing companies on prices.

However, since you now want to enter the market, it is vital to see what prices these companies practice, and what is the average selling price of the products. Setting a higher or lower price brings with it a series of negative consequences for you: on the one hand, additional efforts and benefits are needed for people to buy your products, even if they are more expensive, and on the other hand, you sell a lot, but without profit and then you have no way to last over time.

You see, people love to compare. The satisfaction of finding the best price (careful, I didn't say the lowest), *"getting the best deal"* releases waves of serotonin and dopamine in our body - that's why shopping is a good way to get rid of stress, sadness and anxiety

And it's ridiculous to think that if you list your products in a price comparison, it's like you're suggesting that customers buy from the competition. However, they compare and take into account a lot of factors before making a decision, not just the cost of the product (for example, the brand - do you think people buy iPhones because they have the lowest price?). The ideal is to be somewhere in the middle - to set the prices so that they do not remain fixed, but vary dynamically, depending on the competition and the other factors.

The next factor you take into account in the calculation: costs. And these are not limited to the cost you pay to the supplier or the raw materials, but include all the logistics and marketing costs for selling the product (display on the website, employee salaries, packaging, delivery, etc.).

Calculate the commercial markup according to all these costs and don't play with the profit margin; even though the sales numbers will look great in the reports, soon you won't have the resources, the money, to continue. And customers who only go after the lowest price won't be so understanding if you suddenly want to raise prices.

And if we were still talking about customers, one of the most important factors for the calculation is related to the needs and possibilities of consumers. Psychologically, you can greatly influence the purchase decision, including through price. Thus, you have at your disposal the psychological prices, those that end in other numbers, not necessarily 99 (they are already prohibited for food products) and that give the impression of a lower price due to the reading pattern we use, from left to right.

They work well for short-term, spur-of-the-moment purchases, but for impact purchases, such as a car, round prices are better.

Another method of pricing is adding value through referrals. In other words, if I were to ask you right now how much a half ton hippopotamus costs, you wouldn't be able to give me an answer. But if I tried to sell you a box of toothpicks for 100 euros, you would throw them in my face.

We all have different reference points regarding the cost of a product so a good way to give the impression of a lower cost is to compare it to a common action / object with a lower value.

A third and last method that I will talk about here is to reduce the emotional pain of the consumer when they have to pay. Physically, when you take the money out of your wallet, the excitement of that purchase diminishes. It's like someone putting you in a barrel of cold water.

To reduce this pain and stimulate the desire to buy online, I recommend that you definitely implement card payment. The moment the package arrives at the recipient, he can fully enjoy the product, without being distracted by the fact that he just took out a few hundred lei to give to the courier.

Ultimate eCommerce Masterplan - Nistor Zsolt

And because we're talking about card payment, it's time to move on to choosing payment methods and processors in your online store.

How does the customer pay you?

Did you know that, in Antiquity, stone coins up to 3.5 meters in diameter and weighing 5 tons were used on the island of Yup? Or that salt, spices, tea and cattle were mankind's first money? (Discovera.ro)

I asked you these questions so you can relax after reading this far. But let's get back to the things that interest you.

The choice of payment methods in your store is just as important as the delivery strategy. Maybe it's even more critical because here the client's reason and emotion give the biggest battle.

In principle, the payment methods depend on the type of calo customers you address, but my advice is the more varied, the more People who end up looking at the payment section of the product almost certainly want to buy your product. Maybe they want cash or maybe they want to pay with the credit card or maybe they don't have the whole amount in those, but want to pay in installments. Why should you get in the way of their desire right now, when they are one step away from making the purchase?

Now, depending on the specifics of the products, the costs you are willing to bear, the needs of the customers and so on, implement the most suitable

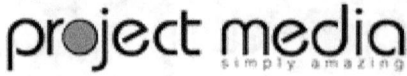

payment method for you: cash / cash on delivery (somewhat mandatory), payment order (increasingly less used), online payment by debit / credit card, payment in installments, advance payment on order, etc.

How to choose the payment processor?

In this step, also pay attention to the integration possibilities in the chosen platform, both as payment methods and at the level of payment processors. If you want to offer card payment, you will need a collaboration with one or more payment processors, and here comes the question of how to choose them.

Payment processing goes hand in hand with the security of the most important data, the personal and banking data of your customers.

You must choose an anti-fraud solution that reduces these risks. In addition to the fact that Google asks us for https sites (with secure protocol) when working with personal data, when the customer is invited to make the payment and enter this data, it will automatically check if the page is secure. If it isn't, most of the time it will go away.

Another security system is 3D Secure, developed by VISA and MasterCard. In this case, both your card and the customer's card must be enrolled in the system.

And to recap, the standard security package when it comes to online payment processing includes a super effective data encryption solution, SSL certificates, billing addresses for all transactions and CVV2 (VISA) or CVC2

(MasterCard) verification - code 3-digit security on the back of the card.

The second thing to think about is the audience you are selling to: local or global? There are solutions for each individual situation. If you want to sell locally, I recommend the country's payment processors, which are already known and credible for this audience.

Talk to them about the specifics of your business, because if you operate in a niche considered risky (gambling, electronic cigarettes, diet programs, etc.) they may not be able to do as much as you would like.

We come to costs again. Payment processors impose certain fees and costs, depending on various criteria: monthly fees, fees as a percentage of the transaction or depending on the volume of the transaction, integration and maintenance costs, cancellation fees, international card payments and so on.

In principle, every processor should have a list of the fees displayed on their website, or if not, you ask them for one. These are closely related to your profit margin - so calculate whether or not you can afford it without affecting your margin. Even if these commissions seem high with the most popular processors on the market, I recommend you also think about their reputation because it will rub off on you, especially the first purchase of a client on the site.

Again, don't run after the lowest price, think 5 times before you go for an obscure promise, low fees, and the like.

Beyond the cost, look at the features / advantages that come with the processor: mobile-ready design when displaying the processing page, if you have possibilities to customize it, automatic communication protocols, if you can set the desired currency and language on the page, which are the refund and stock management services, when you receive your money (what terms / bank settlement files do they offer you), what are the electronic delivery services.

Last but not least, pay attention to the support options they offer you. Sometimes problems arise and the customer can't pay for your order, so it's vital that you get in touch with your payment processor and resolve them as quickly as possible.

Search for opinions, discussions, testimonials and talk to current store owners who already work with the payment processors you want to work with. Find out the strengths and weaknesses of each and only then make a decision.

I consider it sufficient to work with a single payment processor. Even if there are voices that say it's ok to have more and there are stores that offer multiple options in the order completion part, think about the customer. Does he know the difference between them and which one to choose? When you offer too many options, you add thinking time to a decision...time to change your mind.

CUSTOMER SUPPORT

One thing that many tend to forget is the fact that firms, companies do not just mean a name registered at the Trade Register. Companies are what their people / customers make them to be.

In other words, if you or your employees aren't giving them the kind of support they deserve and expect, don't be surprised if no one nominates you for Company of the Year.

When you think about setting up an online store, it's easy to forget details like customer support. But I guarantee you, more than half the time, this task will consume your days and nerves.

People feel a primal need to interact with other people, especially online, if they have doubts or had problems before arriving in your store. Some take this to the extreme, being paranoid about personal data and fear of being stung. This is the truth.

On the other hand, many feel lonely or feel the need to brag. Don't be surprised if people end up keeping you on the phone for tens of minutes or even longer, telling you their whole life, telling you about their problems, worries or the child who is away in Italy and forgot about them.

Or you might find yourself in the awkward position of a psychologist, giving sentimental advice and trying to console / empathize. Customer support is a real palette of thrills that too few warn you about.

Moreover, it is possible to find yourself with some people who simply do not understand. For example, maybe you want to sell wedding favors and, to make them stand out, you also place a set of wedding rings in the product image. Here there is a possibility that people think that they also receive the rings when ordering, although nowhere in the product description do you talk about them. Does it seem unlikely? Trust me, I just gave you a real life example with a real business.

Look, for this very reason, you need to provide good customer support, whether you handle it yourself (although with a large volume of phones, emails and open chat boxes, you won't be able to handle it), or you hire well trained staff.

Now, before we discuss the communication and support channels to use, I want to show you some best practices in dealing with the customer.

First, really listen to him. It's so easy to interrupt someone when they're talking, to point out that you're right, or tell them what they might be missing. But the reality is that there are moments to sell and moments when you have the duty to empathize, to understand the need so as to offer the right solution.

So, when you have to deal with an unsatisfied customer or one who needs a lot of time to formulate his wish, refrain from interrupting him and let him speak his mind until the end. If you see it derails from the topic or goes uphill and downhill, politely steer the conversation back to what you have to share.

Second, put the customer's needs before your own (as long as it's valid). Don't try to sell them as soon as you answer the phone or any other channel, before you know what occasion they called you.

Third, make the customer feel like the number one priority. Even if there are still ten live chat boxes open, respond professionally to each potential customer and be as fast as possible, regardless of the channel - and if you can't respond immediately, give them a time frame in which you will surely come back with an answer.

If you see that you cannot do it yourself, hire more people. Because, you see, it's for nothing that you're advocating multi-channel support if you reply to the customer after a week.

And since we were talking about multi-channel, my recommendation is to provide support on as many channels as possible, with an emphasis on the one you notice that people contact you most often. We are talking about phone, email, live chat, chatbots, Social Media, help center with frequently asked questions and anything else you can think of.

In addition to following good usability practices on all pages of the site, the help center provides answers to the most common possible customer questions (plus it's an always-on type of content).

If you choose to use this option, make sure it's super visible on all pages and also useful to customers. Don't use the help center to talk again about how great your products are, but provide real help, answers that people can actually use, without having to call you or ask you personally on the other channels.

Because the type of support you will provide depends on the specifics of your business (for example, people will call more often if you sell furniture than stationery), I recommend that you think now about what you strictly need for your business.

One important thing to specify. Not all people have to be your customers. If you receive phone calls with threats, the client yells at you and throws egg and vinegar at you, for imaginary reasons, or even if something has happened that concerns you, end the discussion and the relationship with that client as quickly as possible.

Things are exactly the same as the relationship with the team behind the chosen eCommerce platform. Nobody is nobody's slave. And instead of a client who gets on your nerves, insults you and so on, you could interact better with clients who deserve your attention, products and empathy.

Centralize everything in CRM. In translation, Customer Relationship Management represents a joint and tools, procedures and strategies aimed at improving the relationship with customers. It is important to have a history of talking to customers. Thus, new people in your company know everything much faster and become more productive from the very first days.

Even if you respond on several channels to those interested in your products, I recommend you to have a centralization to make a periodic analysis of the situations that have arisen, the words and the approaches used. This way you can make concrete decisions to improve things in your company.

THE 5 ESSENTIAL PAGES FOR A GRADE 10 WEBSITE

Homepage

Now that you have chosen everything related to the technical operation of your store (mainly the platform, because this is where you basically organize the information), it's time to start outlining how it will look.

If in the past the first page mostly meant the customer's first point of contact with the website, today the contact could take place elsewhere. However, the front page still remains the same; this is where the navigation of both the client and the search engines normally begins.

And just like the client view, we'll go with the elements from top to bottom. We start with your store header and placing the most important elements on the first screen (at the top of the screen).

The first element is the logo, which we discussed in a previous chapter. It is located in the left or central part of the page and has the link to the homepage applied.

Next comes the navigation elements, links to category pages and useful information pages - about us, how to buy, how to pay, contact, blog, product warranty if applicable, delivery information, returns, etc. - the latter are usually found in the basement.

Also at the top, place the shopping basket - it must remain visible in whatever page the customer navigates, to encourage the completion of the order, the account authentication form, the contact phone number (on mobile, in the form of click-to- call) and, in general mode, the search box.

I say general mode because the position of the search field can vary, it does not have a fixed location but can be placed differently, depending on the client's needs (it can be in the middle, above or below or it can be placed on the left side) .

You might feel the need to do things differently, change the name of the categories to something creative, place the items differently, whatever, be different. Please don't follow this feeling.

What you see on most sites follows good usability practices and consumer browsing/reading patterns. It's like the way of thinking about seeing pull/push signs on the outside door of a building. We all tend to pull the door to get in.

The moment you, say, place the logo in the lower right or the links to categories in the footer, you are playing on the customers' nerves. They will not realize what site they have reached or how to find the information they are interested in and will leave. You have a different site for nothing if the texture of the information in it is a horror movie played endlessly.

You see, the way the information / elements are arranged in the website emphasizes your unique value proposition, especially on the first page. The same thing must be done by the first banner that the user sees when accessing the page.

You can also use a carousel of images / banners, but it is recommended to eliminate the automatic rotation of the frames and limit them to a maximum of 5 quality images, with a strong call-to-action for each.

Here you can promote the latest offers and news, you can highlight the best-selling products or other benefits that differentiate you from the competition. It is also important to mention the extra benefits for the consumer: free shipping or free shipping after a certain order value, extended return period, warranty, free packaging, shorter delivery time, etc.

Regarding the chromatics, my recommendation is to be consistent. Reduce the colors used to 4-5, and make sure that the call-to-action buttons contrast with the background - but have the same color on all pages. Consistency will make the user recognize the button they can click, regardless of the page.

Further down the page, people are generally used to the presentation of discounted or new products. Highlight them by displaying specific marketing marks, but, be careful, do not apply them to all products, to avoid the effect of banner blindness. In the same vein, avoid boxes, border lines, or any other type of elements that load the design unnecessarily.

Evidence of credibility such as guarantees, trust marks, logos of payment processors and media outlets (if applicable), testimonials and customer ratings are just as important.

For those who have not yet decided to buy, provide different ways to stay in touch (turn them into leads): post links to your Social Media pages and invite them to subscribe to your newsletter / blog of the company. An interesting idea is to automate the display of the latest blog articles on the front page of the site. Thus, the first page is constantly updated, representing a strong positive signal for Google.

Obviously, we have not forgotten the SEO part, but we will discuss this in a later chapter dedicated to the subject.

Product page

People want to know what they are buying. Products with a higher price need more detailed presentations.

Give every reason for people to buy from you. Towards the end I will teach you how you can speed up this sales process through the bidding mode.

Any product page in your online store can account for over 70% of your sales funnel, concurrently or not. Here you can attract attention, stimulate interest and desire for the user to take action (according to the A.I.D.A. model). It rarely happens that the user buys on the first interaction with your website or product page, but allegorically it should at least be able to attract attention.

Here we will not talk about the header, since it remains on the "First page. And to end the discussion, the header remains the same in all pages of the site, with the exception of the shopping cart and checkout page.

The first defining element for the product page is the name of the product, or the title of the product, in full, with a larger size than the rest of the font, bold and delimited by white spaces. Under it, optionally, you can place the rating or note of the product.

The second element is the product image/images. I recommend using large, quality images that show the product from all possible angles, with absolutely all the details. You get extra points from the consumer if you also present the product in context, because that way they can figure out the approximate size and how it looks when used.

For example, it would be ridiculous to have a fashion site and present images of the products on the hanger. Man has no way of getting an idea of how the dressed product looks. Or, if you sell, for example, satchels and bags, as well, present them - and - on a model.

It offers the zoom function, so that users can see even the smallest details, but pay attention to the size of the images - the larger they are, the slower the loading speed of the site will be. An alternative would be to use 360-degree images and product videos.

In the same line as the first elements, in the first screen (at the top), place a short commercial description of the product (the most important benefits for the customer), information about stock availability or the option "ask stock" or stock alert (for the moment in that the product is back on sale), the option to select attributes (size, color, technical specifications, etc.), information about delivery costs or free shipping and other trust benefits (warranty, return, money back, payment in installments, points fidelity).

Legally and in common sense you must also display the price of the product here, including the full discounted price, if it has been reduced. Immediately below it you place the catalyst of the action - the "Add to cart" button. It is recommended to keep the language as natural as possible, not to pressure the consumer to buy, with imperatives such as "buy now", "order now" or any other wording that does not imply freedom of choice.

Keep the same color for call-to-action buttons descriptive press for what happens on click. Your website users don't have to be like Dee Dee from Dexter's Lab *"ooh what does the button do?"* - BOOM - but he must know what effect the click on that button will have.

In addition to the commercial description, it also displays a technical description of the product but avoids jargon and complex terms. Maybe for you they are as familiar as hello, but don't start from this premise; create descriptions like for third graders.

If you have product reviews, display them on the page, whether positive or negative. Exactly, and the negative ones - they are a signal of confidence for customers, because they are also aware that if it sounds too good to be true, it is.

Allow your customers to give you reviews and keep an eye on this section. If you see a negative review, a question or any other type of comment that requires your intervention, interact with the customer and answer them, offer them a solution, so that you can win them over. You will surely win: maybe an idea for optimizing the page, the product or the offer comes to you that you never even thought of.

Other elements that can be found on the product page to stimulate the sale or to increase the average value of the order are the complementary / accessory products, the list of previously viewed products, emergency elements and FOMO (countdown until the expiration of an offer, highlighting of limited stock , highlighting the benefit of faster delivery on immediate order, etc.).

Checkout page

The checkout page on your website is where the magic happens. Sometimes magic just doesn't happen, and that's a bigger wake-up call than a cold shower in the morning.

Good practices (and common sense) tell us to remove from the page any extra element that could distract the customer from the action we want him to do: fill in the order data and complete it.

For this reason we stated that the standard header disappears on the checkout page. Ideally, the logo, contact details and benefits / evidence of trust that drives the order remain at the top. Instead of categories, you can display links to the first page (optional, since it can also be accessed by clicking on the logo), to the help center, my account, testimonials, pages with useful information, etc. Choose the links carefully, only the most important ones for the specifics of your business.

To give security to the customer, here it is mandatory to display the entire content of the shopping cart: name, product thumbnail, ply the chosen attributes, quantity (which can be modified), trend costs (which you also displayed on the product page), subtotal and total cost.

If you choose a platform or take care of configuring the order form yourself, limit the number of fields to fill in, highlight the mandatory / optional ones and do not ask for sensitive information that only you need to create the marketing client profile. This is not the right time or place, because you will alarm the client and he will abandon the process.

Also, if errors occur or the customer forgets to fill in a mandatory field, report the error to them immediately, don't wait for them to press the "send / complete the order" button.

Another element is the customer's account. On the one hand, an account is a real treasure for you - you can customize it and your marketing offers to infinity. But there are customers who are in a hurry or who simply don't want / don't feel like creating an account.

For this reason, it also allows ordering without an account.

Very important: do not automatically check the boxes, agree to your store's terms and conditions and subscribe to the newsletter.

Display your evidence of credibility, including testimonials from satisfied customers. And so. If you want the person to do other actions (give you a review, follow you on social networks, etc.), save your intent for the thank you / order confirmation page.

To facilitate the next order made by an existing customer at your online store, automatically fill in the form fields with the information you already have and save him from wasting time.

I don't think there is any point in discussing the security of the checkout page - for an online store it is mandatory to implement an SSL certificate, secure payment and order processing and display a confirmation that the customer's personal data is safe.

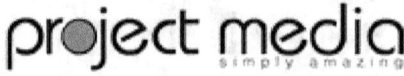

About us page

This is about your business or you, not the products you sell.

As I've said many times, people buy from you when they trust you. And trust must be earned.

In this section you must tell and show who you are, your story and the why behind the business. Why do you think you can revolutionize the niche industry, why you can become the best in the market in the next 3 years.

You've probably heard a lot of stories on the Internet about customers who ordered phones and received potatoes. Well, no one likes to be tricked, which is why people quickly check the seller before making a purchase decision.

Do you know what the online equivalent of a business card is? That's right, the "about us" page of your online store. This is not exactly the first point of contact with the customer, but it is a strong testimony that you are human, that there are real people behind the curtain that you can interact with and who are doing everything in their power to meet the pressing need .

This is the right place to tell your story honestly and trace the desired brand culture. For this reason, giving up expressions like "the best" , "best quality products", "the best" really works with the customer.

Sometimes I sit and think and it seems so ridiculous to see sites addressed in the second person, plural. It's as if they imagine that people are sitting in a group in front of the computer or the phone and that's how they make the purchase decision.

Yes, you have several customers (ideally), but each customer buys in turn, for him (or, please, also for others, but he alone clicks the button, not all at once). Talk to your client in a conversational style, without bombastic expressions and attempts to be polite. Don't take him with you, you want to be friends.

Now that we've dealt with the style of writing on the about us page (and the rest of the site), let's see what it should contain.

First, your story, of your company. Simply tell him what led you to open the store, what stages you went through, how you arrived at the right solution for what needs he has and what stage you are at now.

How to approach the story depends on the specifics of your business. Do you sell funny products / do you like a funny approach? Then entertain your client. Do you sell more serious products? Don't get lost in the cornfield, but keep a professional tone, combining personal elements with customer benefits.

Also here you can tell him about your products, where they come from, how they were created and other beneficial features for him.

Confidently use photos / videos from behind the curtain, alone or with the team (possibly place the last posts on the agram here), present certificates, diplomas or any other distinctions you have won and customer testimonials (what are more strongly accompanied by photos).

Don't hide your team, if you have employees. Introduce them to the world, let them get to know them and even follow them on LinkedIn if they want - so the process of adapting the customer to the brand culture can continue, beyond the actual website. Moving on to a utility element, it displays the exact position of the company's headquarters on the map, along with identification data, addresses, phone and email numbers, as well as the contact schedule.

After all this information, you can direct users to a specific landing with an offer, you can invite them to subscribe to the newsletter / blog, to follow you on different social networks or any other page, on which you want to draw attention.

Never leave users hanging. Don't expect them to go from the about us page to a category or the front page of the site on their own. You show them the best way and you kill two birds with one stone: they don't have to scroll up and down / waste time anymore and you direct them to the hottest place for you.

For visitors to your store who have reached this section and had the patience to see all the information about your company, you can display a unique discount code below the page, which can be applied in different situations and which you can monitor.

In a crowded world of brands, with many ads and notifications from social media that disrupt our focus, transparency, unique communication style and customer experience make the difference and help you grow.

Contact page

Yes, maybe you expected me to talk about the category or thank you page, but here I am addressing both online stores with products and services. Whatever category you fall into, the contact page is vital for the operation of the store; and I mean, first of all, the trust factor.

If on the about us page you establish an emotional connection with the customer and he gets to know you better, on the contact page the connection takes place physically, in the discussion with you / your team. If you make the mistake of displaying a contact form and that's it, you probably haven't done the following imaginary exercise: *"Let me ask them if I can order 50 units of product x at a discount. Oh look, just a contact form. Why doesn't he tell me where the company headquarters are? Why won't you give me more details? It sure is cool!"*

Done with imagining? See why you should pay attention to this page? Let's see what are the must-have elements for your online store's contact page.

First of all, you must display the complete data of your company, the contact data, the assistance program, specific information for the business, for example, if you also have a physical location, display the operating hours of the happy hour with promotions, display the time interval respectively etc.).

He also adds the name and photo of the contact persons (the support person, the sales person or anyone else), so he knows from the start who he will talk to, who answers his phone or email. This helps a lot to relax the client and promotes communication.

Then, place on the page the map with the position of your headquarters (use Google Maps), as well as links to the Social Media pages, so that you can be contacted directly on those pages.

As for the standard contact form, limit the number of fields to fill in and, if you can, mark the phone number field as optional. Likewise, limit the send message button to just one.

Don't be too generous with the buttons, give him a "delete message" button because he might hit it by mistake. I think you can imagine the nerves created if he accidentally deletes the text he intended to send you.

Last but not least, automatically confirm that their message has been received and that they will receive a reply as soon as possible. It's frustrating to be unsure (did it send, didn't it send) so save the user a worry and show the confirmation message as soon as they hit the send button.

Alternatively, after completing the form, you can direct people to a thank you landing page, where you can offer them a guide or an extra benefit, so that you can start the process of familiarization and attraction to your brand. This increases your chances of converting the contact into a buyer.

How do you like it so far? You are curious what you have to do next! Well get ready, you're about to find out the steps involved in launching an online store, including the necessary marketing tactics that I'm sure you're looking forward to.

WANT A TOP NOTCH WEBSITE? USE THE CHECKLIST

Design

1. **The website design is responsive**. The website pages are compatible with most devices - PC, tablets, mobile phones, Android, iPhone, etc.
2. **The website pages are compatible with most browsers** used by users (Internet Explorer, Chrome, Firefox, Safari, Opera, Edge)
3. **You have carefully chosen your domain**, with an address that is easy to remember, short and easily distinguishable from those available online.
4. **CSS/HTML is properly validated**.
5. **Scripts are optimized on all pages**.
6. **Images are small in size to load quickly**.

Accessibility

1. **The page load time is reasonable** - according to statistics, the right time is 2-3 seconds or less.
2. **Adequate contrast between the text and the background image** used on the site - eyes and monitors

differ, so make sure that people can easily read the content of the site.

3. **The size of the fonts and the space between the words is reasonable** - choose an easy-to-read font and a suitable size, so that people can read the texts easily. Keep in mind that small/too large text leads to frustration, and frustration leads to site abandonment.

4. **Watch out for plugins or other programs** - users won't wait forever for them to load. Use them carefully only if they make a real contribution to the site's objective.

5. **Images have relevant Alt-text** - so that search engine spiders can understand/index those images, but also to be understood by the user, if the images do not load on the site.

6. **Site has a custom 404 page** - this error usually leads to user frustration and site abandonment. Be sure to customize it by providing navigation options to other pages to direct people to your content.

Functionality

1. The **forms on the website correctly capture the entered data**.
2. T**hank you messages or thank you pages are displayed** after the completed form is submitted to the database.
3. **Form data is sent by email to a secure address** or stored in a database.
4. **Autoresponders work properly** - if you use these tools to simplify your marketing strategies, time and effort invested.

5. **The internal links in the site work correctly**.
6. **External links from the site, to other sites, work correctly** and open in a new tab.
7. **Social share icons work properly**.
8. **Feeds work properly** - news, news, social media, etc.
9. **Integrations with third parties such as CRM applications, ERE, eCommerce software, marketing automation applications work correctly** and do not affect the site in any way.

Identity

1. The site **logo is placed on all pages** in the same place, as visible as possible - usually it is placed in the upper left, the place where people are already used to finding it.
2. **Use a slogan/motto that conveys the essence of the site** - tell the user what you do or what you can help them with, in a short sentence that is, in fact, your unique selling proposition (USP).
3. **The first page of the site is easy to consume, in 5 seconds** - in other words, the user must understand in less than 5 seconds what he has to gain in your site.
4. **Ensure an easy way to get to the About Us page** - whether you have an online business, a blog, a news site or any other type of site, you need a page where you can present information about yourself or your company . People feel the need to know who they are interacting with in order to trust them.
5. **You provide an easy way to get to the Contact page** - think that maybe people want to contact you, even if you

don't sell anything with your site. So give them contact information so they can get in touch with you. If you have an online store, in addition to the email address, a phone number is mandatory.

Navigation

1. **The main menu bar is visible** - displaying a navigation hint so that people can easily figure out how to get to the desired pages and what is the structure of the site - for example, if you have an eCommerce site, create a category for the main products you sell.
2. **Category labels are short and easy to understand** - not Let's talk about how many great things we can do in ng when "Contact" or "Contact us" is enough for the user to understand what he has to do.
3. **The number of links is reasonable** - if you want to have 7 or more categories, think first if they really need them. Consider the variety of products you sell, if you have an eCommerce site, or the variety of categories you write for, blog/online newspaper, etc.
4. **Users know where they are at all times** - use a secondary navigation menu such as breadcrumbs or a sitemap.
5. **The site logo is linked to the front page** - no matter how small this detail may seem to you, people are already used to the logo leading to Home and if they don't have this functionality, you're just giving them more things.
6. **Links are consistent and easy to identify** - users are used to links being blue or underlined. Don't try to

reinvent the wheel, you'll just confuse them. Also, do not abuse the number of links in the text.

7. **Have a search box on the site, easy to access** - keep the button as simple and concise as possible.

SEO - optimizing for search engine results (Google)

1. **Choose www or non-www** to make sure it just works and you won't be penalized for duplicate content.
2. **Pages have unique titles** - less than 70 characters including your chosen keywords of 70 characters, including the chosen keyword.
3. **Pages have unique meta descriptions** - less than 155 characters, including keywords.
4. **Pages are optimized** around relevant keywords.
5. You have **correctly placed the metas for any content** shared on social networks.
6. You **spell-checked and grammar-checked the metas**.
7. You have **added relevant alt-text to the images used**.
8. You have **created a dynamic XML sitemap** - that is, it updates automatically when new content appears.
9. You have **listed the XML sitemap in the robots.txt** file
10. You have **submitted your XML sitemap to Google Search Console**.
11. **Page URLs are short** and reflect the content on those pages.
12. **You made a 301 redirect** for products without stock, to similar products.

13. **You applied rel="nofollow"** tags to all links and pages where needed.

Content

1. **You have created relevant text content** for the site and checked it for spelling and grammar. The most important content is placed above the fold - visible without the user having to scroll.
2. **Headings, paragraphs and lists are clear**, descriptive and use appropriate font types and sizes on all website pages.
3. **The copyright date is placed in the footer** and includes the current year.
4. **Contact details are correct and visible throughout the site**.
5. **Generic content displayed prior to site launch** (such as lorem ipsum) has been removed and replaced.
6. **Images, videos and audio files are placed in the right places**, are edited and work on any device.
7. **Have a call-to-action button on every page of the site**.
8. **Any premium content** (guides, ebooks, case studies) is stored in a secure base and works as it should.
9. If you have an online business, you are trying to sell something with your website, **you have displayed the price of the products/services** in a visible and accessible place.

Analytics

1. **The Google Analytics code has been inserted** in all pages of the site, correctly.
2. **Internal IP addresses have been excluded** from monitoring
3. You've **created funnels and goals in your Analytics** software - this is a step specifically for eCommerce sites.
4. You **have correctly linked the Google Analytics account with the Search Console account**.
5. You **have correctly linked the Google Analytics account with the Google Ads account** - if you choose to promote your site through paid advertisements.

Security

1. You have **24/7 monitoring scripts installed**
2. You **use SSL security certificates** - and not just for eCommerce sites, if you store and process credit cards or confidential information
3. You **made a backup after the last version of the website**
4. You **make copies of the latest versions of the website** regularly and store them somewhere safe.
5. **Site passwords and confidential user information are stored on secure servers**

Compliance Specifications

1. The website announces if it **uses cookies and asks for GDPR consent - mandatory by law**.

2. The **terms and conditions are visible** to website visitors.
3. You **have a privacy policy page**, it is linked to all forms where you request data and is visible on all website pages.
4. The **site complies with PCI compliance terms** - if it is an eCommerce site that stores and processes credit card data.
5. **Publishing rights for images**, fonts or other content are mentioned as protected or quoted.

LAUNCHING AN ONLINE BUSINESS

The most important thing to do in any business is take action as quickly as possible.

Too much holding back, brooding, and protracted discussions about ideas do nothing but leave room for your competitors to grow.

The idea is to enter the market, launch your business as quickly as possible. You can take advantage of all the information you get in this book.

And now tell me, how do you want to launch your online store? Oh yes, live events, on Facebook, discounts, etc., etc.

When I ask about the launch strategy of an online store, many tend to think strictly about the practical campaigns they will do on launch day. But wait a minute, let me ask you something.

How will people find you on Google? Or on Facebook or other networks? How are you going to maintain the relationship with them once they give you contact information? How are you going to keep them entertained, keep them coming?

It's easy to see only the top, glazed with caramelized sugar and adorable customers eager to enter the store and buy. But the strategy of launching an online business requires a real deployment of forces, which starts a few weeks before the actual launch and continues over time.

Because, you see, you can imagine yourself making a real launch every time your business name comes to the attention of a new customer.

Therefore, in this chapter we will discuss some essential marketing concepts for the visibility of your store.

Remember, you can't create a store and wait for customers to fall from the sky. Customers must be enticed and encouraged, both to enter the store and to stay and buy.

Imagine a situation like this: you have invested a lot of time to build the interior of your store. Inside is luxury, everything is arranged as per the book, the bulbs shine charmingly, and the products are creatively and attractively organized. It's just that... from the outside, your shop building is dilapidated, with crumbling walls and boarded-up windows.

Well, that's exactly how your online store looks to customers if you don't have visibility in front of them. When you're not on social media or sitting somewhere on page 5 of Google, it's like trying to sell from a run-down house.

SEARCH ENGINE OPTIMIZATION (SEO) STRATEGY

As a human species, today we are at the highest point of evolution. Thanks to electricity, technology evolves at an incredible speed, which gives us instant access to any information in different formats: text, video, audio or images.

Practically this makes us smarter. We already know how to work with data, with information, we know how to search, compare things, and we are also learning to filter the source of information.

Consuming content / information has become a daily habit for the billions of people with access to the Internet, and in most cases it all starts with looking for a solution to a problem.

Google has become the most reliable partner for us and helps us reach the desired information quickly. The search engine is based on one of the most powerful algorithms in the world, which evolves daily.

Knowing the searches that are made, the time of day, month or year, devices - mobile, tablet or PC, location and much more, with the help of AI (Artificial Intelligence) and Machine learning systems, this algorithm came to know more information about us, than we think we know.

I am convinced that in most situations, when you did a Google search, you received relevant results.

You can help clients find your business in the first positions in the search engine if you go through an entire optimization process - SEO (Search Engine Optimization)

SEO - a concept and a job as much discussed as it is confusing For most future entrepreneurs, SEO seems more important than the actual sale to the customer. Oh yes, we met many at the agency who, at first, told us they wanted marketing or SEO, and after a few days they started asking: why am I not the first in Google?

Why don't I have sales?!

Simply put, SEO or search engine optimization strategy is a long-term marketing strategy. Even Google representatives said that you need at least 6-8 months for results.

Now you might be saying *"ok, then why invest DEO resources when I'm interested in the immediate results?"* Well, they help you in the long run, getting higher and higher in Google.

Plus, ethical SEO techniques respect search engine regulations and protect you from penalties.

SEO is like a marriage. You don't immediately get married / married to Google, like in real life on the first date (maybe only if you are vegas dust), and the baby (results) is not born immediately, it also needs 9 months to develop.

If you have minimal on-page optimization or minimal SEO knowledge, you can take care of on-page or even off-page optimization yourself or, if not, call a specialized agency / freelancer. But it is important to prioritize your goals.

The purpose of doing SEO is not to reach number 1 in Google, but to have sales and conversions. The two things are not necessarily correlated, so focus on a commercial optimization strategy, on commercial keywords.

SEO Audit from A to Z

Basically, any SEO strategy should start with an audit. It accounts for the existing elements and traces the optimization direction you will follow.

I think you realize what's coming now. I'll show you how to practically do an SEO audit of your site and as you find out what elements you're missing / need to change, adjust them in real time, from choosing the most suitable keywords to meta tags, link building strategy and technical checks.

Now, I will go through this audit step by step. Before we get started, I want to make sure you're familiar with some terms and tools. As long as you follow the instructions, you should be fine.

First, we have the technical jargon with terms like URL (specifies the web address of a file, in this case the addresses of your pages), robots.txt (file that tells search engine robots what they can access or not in a site), metas or meta tags (HTML elements inserted in the website code, to provide information or instructions - according to Wikipedia), dofollow and nofollow attributes (HTML attributes that inform search engines that the link should influence the ranking in the index, respectively don't influence it), backlink (link from other pages or sites sent to your main page or domain). Obviously, there are others, but I will explain them along the way.

Secondly, you will use some specific SEO tools for on-page and off-page analysis such as cognitive SEO, Ahrefs, Google Keyword Planner, Google Search Console (make an account as soon as possible), SEMrush, etc. Some are free up to a certain point, some are premium. Now, lastly, it also depends on the platform if you will need technical knowledge for changes in the site.

If we have clarified these things, let's move on to the actual analysis. Any SEO audit consists of three major areas: the technical part, on-page (content, information architecture, keywords) and off-page (link building, Social Media, competitors, brand mentions).

Careful! If you've just put your website live, you won't find it immediately in Google, no matter what keyword you're looking for. It will appear somewhere in the results provided only after it is indexed by the search engine, which takes a while.

I felt the need to add this because my support colleagues told me they've spoken to customers who couldn't understand why they couldn't find their site right away.

Technical SEO Audit

Even if the term *"technical"* seems to scare everyone, using Search Console, Screaming Frog and the other tools at your disposal, the job becomes much simpler.

The first technical thing you need to check is your DNS server configuration and domain settings so that search engine bots don't run into errors when crawling your site.

What are the rules here? The robots.txt file must be configured correctly, allow pages to be indexed and hide those that are still being worked on or contain sensitive information.

Next, the sitemap or sitemap.xml file must be added to the Search Console account, so that it leads to rapid indexing, indicating to Google spiders the architecture and pages of your site. In the same line, the location of the map should be indicated from the robots.txt file (also to help with indexing). You can create the map using the XML Sitemaps Generator.

As we said in the previous chapters, the encrypted protocol (https instead of http) is mandatory for an online store. If you still have http, redirect it to secure pages.

Regarding the redirects you have to do, if necessary, redirect 301 and not 302 (in the case of temporary redirects, Google may consider the page as duplicate content), and if you have several domain variants (http://store .com, http://www.store.com, https://store.com, https://www.store.com), redirect to the domain you want indexed, either www or non-www.

Also, if you have pages with similar content but different URLs, implement the rel=canonical tag to indicate the base / main page to display and thus avoid duplicate content (often happens in the case of online stores, from filters and result pages on an internal search).

Last but not least, pay close attention to 404 errors (page not found) or other broken links. In the event that the user types in the wrong URL or encounters a 404, customize the page and make sure they can still navigate your site.

Part technical and part design, one thing to check is your site's loading speed. A load time greater than 2-3 seconds generally decreases the consumer's experience and pushes them away to other sites.

Plus, the increased bounce rate that results from this causes search engines to rank you much lower on the results page. Check your load speed using Pingdom or Google PageSpeed Insights.

There are some standard reasons that can lead to slow loading times such as the ratio of text to code (too much code), page size (over 1.5 MB slows you down), image size (compress them), caching, etc. Also talk to the developer, if necessary, to remove, minimize or outsource the misplaced parts of the code.

Now that we've discussed accessibility factors, both for search engine bots and customers, it's time to get back to indexability.

The first thing to do is launch a "site:magazin.ro" command. See the number of search results returned and compare it to the number displayed in Search Console. It is normal that they are not identical, but if you see a huge difference, it is necessary to explore the reasons why you were not indexed properly (maybe you were penalized, maybe you have duplicate content, etc.).

The next vital element (seriously, I don't know why we didn't discuss this sooner) is optimizing your design for mobile. Mainly, I mean the need for a responsive design, which adapts regardless of the size of the screen used. To see how mobile-friendly you are, use Google's Mobile-Friendly Test.

Also, create a Google Analytics account, implement the tracking code in all pages of your website and activate the Enhanced Ecommerce function. And if you also have a physical location, an outlet, headquarters or shop, create a Google My Business account and fill it in with all your data.

Last but not least, my advice is to use structured data. These describe the things in the site, along with their properties. Using them, your content will appear in more attractive results for customers, with images, rating stars, extensions, etc.

CHECKLIST CHECKING THE ACCESSIBILITY OF YOUR ONLINE STORE

You've scanned the site with Cognitive SEO (or another tool) to uncover potential issues, including indexing and crawling.

You have a Search Console account or have created one right now.

You have linked your Google Search Console account with your Google Analytics account.

Your site loads faster than 2 seconds (check using https://tools.pingdom.com/).

You used the site:domeniultău.ro command to manually check the number of pages indexed in Google.

You then check in Google Search Console the number of indexed pages, see if there are any big differences (possible duplicate content, maybe some pages are blocked with robots.txt, etc.).

Check the robots.txt files and take care to restrict access to pages with sensitive information (use example.ro/robots.txt or Google Search Console to check).

You use the Crawl Errors report in Search Console to find potential 40x errors.

You use the Crawl Errors > Other report in Search Console to find potential 50x errors.

You check the XML sitemap (with example.ro/sitemap.xml or Search Console), and if you don't have one yet, you create it using an online generator and then add it to your Search Console account.

You also have an image sitemap added to Search Console.

If applicable, have a mobile sitemap added to Search Console.

If you have a lot of videos, generate a video sitemap that you add to your Search Console account.

You have checked the 404 error pages and customized them to direct users to other pages on your site (check example.ro/shfkld)

You have structured your site with the help of breadcrumbs (secondary navigation (if you have more categories)

You have verified that there is a link on the website logo and, optionally, Alt-text complete with the name of the website.

You use structured data on the site (Schema.org) and you have tested their implementation (use https://developers.google.com/structured-data/testing-tool)

You use the footer of the site to place links to non-commercial pages (about us, frequently asked questions, how to buy, how to pay, etc.)

Use short, clean URLs, less than 100 characters, and if you have to separate words in URLs, use a hyphen, not another symbol.

You have completed the meta tags in each page of your site, unique, using keywords.

If it is necessary to redirect, choose redirect 301 instead of 302 because you know that Google may not index the page considering that it is a temporary action.

You do 301 redirects to 404 pages, where a lot of traffic comes.

Check that you don't have broken redirects that lead to pages with errors.

You checked the volume of links with rel=nofollow and rel=dofollow.

You have a Google My Business profile for your business, especially if it also has a physical location.

You have installed an SSL certificate, and your website secures the data collected from leads and customers.

Your site is prepared for the needs of mobile users (use https://search.google.com/test/mobile-friendly)

Every time you update the content, you send a re-indexing request to the Search Console account so that the search engine robots visit the page faster.

KEYWORD MINI-AUDIT: HOW TO CHOOSE THE BEST KEYWORDS

Phew, tired of the technical part? Well, you're fed up just in time because I just want to jump into the process of keyword discovery and analysis. Take a break from technique for now.

I start with this part because, based on the keywords, you will create the metas and other details related to on-page optimization. On top of that, the subject of keywords grinds the majority of entrepreneurs, all of them are hunting for the most profitable words to beat the competition and attract the client to their site.

The classic procedure of choosing the best key terms is no longer, I think, valid. Changes such as the appearance of updates in the Google algorithm, Hummingbird, Panda penalties, Penguin, Mobilegeddon and the implementation of artificial intelligence - RankBrain, have led to the transformation of the approach from head terms / exact, short keywords to long tail keywords and an emphasis on semantics.

Imagine Google as a child. When he goes to school and reads from the textbook, ideally he should learn as easily as possible and understand the information. If it is not optimized for the child's needs (with images, naturally structured information and a pleasant, attractive experience), he will not be able to understand anything. It works exactly the same way at the user level.

When you start the process of choosing keywords, you need to be aware that you are not only doing this to find favorable phrases for SEO, not only for Google, but also to understand the needs, wants and search patterns used by potential customers - those who are most interested in what you sell.

In short, we classify keywords into two main categories: short-tail, short / exact words (*"dresses"*, *"refrigerator"*, *"motorcycle"*, etc.) and long-tail, longer phrases, which translate a higher purchase intent (*"winter tires for vw polo 1996", "running shoes size 40", "wood burning stove free shipping"* etc.).

Now, it seems somewhat logical that the person searching for *"shoes"* might fall into a wide range of interests (maybe doing a project about shoes, maybe looking for pictures of shoes, maybe wanting to see what kind of shoes are out there.), as opposed to by the one searching for *"running shoes size 40"*. The latter falls within a narrow area of interests: either they want to buy, or they want to document themselves on the offer on the market in the event of a purchase.

You see, over 70% of Google searches in a day are represented by long-tail keywords although in much smaller numbers than general keywords. To reconcile the goat and the cabbage, my advice is to focus on the long-tail from the start, without forgetting the general terms; you rank faster on the long tail, but you must also optimize for the short tail, for the results of which you will have to wait longer.

So how do you find the right keywords for your online business?

First, think about the words and phrases that potential customers might use to search. Also remember when you searched for your product in Google, to see who the competitors are or if it exists on the market.

Create a new table in Excel / Google Drive and start writing down keywords that come to your mind, similar searches shown at the bottom of a Google search, specific words for category / product pages, which you already have on your site, keywords plus the name of your store, synonyms and words from the same semantic field, etc. Also take into account the phrases or words used by current customers of the competition on forums, Social Media and other groups.

Then, to validate the list of ideas made so far, but also to find new words, use the tools available online: Google Keyword Planner (you will need a Google Ads account), Keyword Tool, Ubersuggest, Google Trends, cognitiveSEO (function for keywords it's super developed and helps you optimize your content to the maximum), SEMrush, MOZ, etc.

Choose which tool you want from the list and use it. Some of these give you additional data such as competition, monthly search volume, and more.

Yes, and since we were talking about the competition, take a look at these companies as well. Not because I urge you to use the same words and focus on their optimization (at least not from the first), but because that way you can discover optimization opportunities on the words ignored by them.

It's vital to understand this: not everything the competition does is good for you. If you want to shoot hard from the start on the words of the competition, you will see that you will not be able to beat them in positions, especially if they already have authority and seniority behind them.

No matter how well optimized your competition is, a site validated by consumers through trust, low bounce rate, time spent on pages, authority and seniority will be ranked higher by search engines. Defeating them is a difficult road, easier only if you have a different approach and gain more confidence.

To conclude on keywords, add to the list possible expressions or phrases that users would use to reach your business: a specific example, *"how do I choose the best office chair"*, *"where do I find office chairs ergonomics"*, *"what kind of office chair should I choose"*, *"ergonomic office chair for home"*, etc.

ON-Page SEO Audit

Keep your keyword list handy because you will use it to the maximum to optimize your website pages.

We start with the features of the main page navigation menu, which, even if you didn't expect it, are critical for SEO, since they influence the customer experience. Make sure that the user can reach the main sections of the site in a maximum of 2 clicks, 6-7 categories displayed in the bar (otherwise they tire the eyes), are arranged logically and consist of keywords, descriptive (short expressions).

At the opposite pole we have the navigation at the bottom of the page, which must provide useful information, be logical in accordance with the main navigation menu and strategic (usually here you present the contact and identification data of the company).

As for website URLs, they should be as short as possible, descriptive and include the main keyword of each individual page. Do not exceed a maximum of 100 characters and use hyphens instead of underscores "_" to separate words.

If you use breadcrumbs - bookmarks for the user's navigation path in the site (and I recommend them if you have many categories and products), make sure that they are functional and visible at the top of the site.

If until now it seems to you that I have talked about small details in on-page optimization, know that you are right. This was just a warm-up for what's to come: optimizing every page on the site, starting from the homepage to the last one.

The first element is the meta title, unique for each page, which includes the main keyword, does not exceed 70 characters (it also depends on Google's directives, it may change), is relevant and can include calls to action / verbs to the imperative.

The second is the meta-description, likewise, unique for each page, includes the main keyword, but also similar products / terms from the same semantic field, does not exceed 158 characters and is an attractive description for potential customers.

You know the bench with an SEO dude walking into a bar, bars, restaurant, restaurants, pub, tavern, beer, whiskey...? Well, don't do that with your meta description or the rest of your website content. Do not do keyword stuffing - a spam tactic in which you stuff as many keywords as possible into the content, their density exceeding 80% of the text. Use as natural a language as possible, which attracts the consumer.

Furthermore, each page has completed H1 (at least), H2, H3 and so on, basically the headings and subheadings that organize the information on the page from the most important to the least important, using the main keywords.

Regarding on-page keyword density, because I skipped this topic, the point is that there is no fixed rule. What is critical, however, is to be as natural as possible in the placement or repetition of keywords and rather use their semantic alternatives.

How long should the content be on the page? I get this question a lot, and likewise, the answer varies depending on the relevance to the consumer and their needs. Do you need to explain in detail, give additional information so that the user understands everything? Then write more.

Is a text of 400 words enough to talk about your business without the need to repeat yourself? Then keep it to 400 words and don't fill up the space for nothing. But before you settle for 400 words, do a quick Google search on your target keywords to see the differences between your content VS those in the top 5 positions. Go ahead, I guess you know what to do :)

As for the type of content, make sure it's relevant to the consumer and unique, original, yours - whatever you want to call it. Don't just take the descriptions from the supplier, slap them on the product pages because that's what everyone does. Stand out with unique descriptions - avoid duplicate content penalties and rank higher in the results.

Ultimate eCommerce Masterplan - Nistor Zsolt

What do you do when you have hundreds, thousands of products? You start with the top products, which you want to sell the best, and the products on the offer pages, and over time, you can take care of the others one at a time - or outsource their creation.

Make sure that the architecture of the information is easy to understand on the pages and use readable fonts, different sizes to prioritize the information, supported by the browser, as well as white spaces, contrasting colors, etc. Do a test with your eyes half open: can you tell what the most important points on the page are? If not, you should work on the layout and design.

Fixed, technical elements will always matter less to Google if people validate you through extended site page visits and trust.

Just to encourage repeat visits and interactivity on the page, it is advisable to constantly update the content. Since you are still in the launch phase of the store, I recommend you to remember for later: try to update the content of each page at least once a year.

Also for attractiveness and interactivity, in terms of SEO you need multimedia elements in the site - images, infographics, videos, gifs, etc. Don't forget to change the names of the images with some descriptive / keywords and fill in the Alt-text attribute (it will display suggestive information about the image when hovering over it or if it hasn't fully loaded).

You should know the following about internal links: you only use them if they are relevant to the user and if they really help to continue navigating the site to useful pages. Regarding their number, from Google you can have 100 links on the page, as long as you respect what I told you previously. However, avoid building blocks of internal links in the footer of pages, it will be a spam signal.

As for links going from your site to other pages or main domains, be very careful who you befriend. Linking to sites specific to your niche, with authority and seniority, can help you optimize, but not if you don't mind linking to sites disapproved or penalized by Google.

Because you are at the beginning, if you have many products, I recommend that you focus on the most important pages on the site and possibly the pages with the products that you predict will sell the best. In time, you have time to optimize the rest as well.

Off-Page SEO Audit

Who recommends your products and how?

Do you remember the guy who washed your car last time? If you wash your car at the same place, you are probably satisfied with the services you receive and trust them, which is very good.

The new iPhone model has just been released, you would like to buy it, but you want to know more technical information about it. What do you think the chances are that the person who is very good at cleaning cars will help you with such information? How believable can they be? Well... not really.

But if you ask him for recommendations on a solution that removes chocolate stains from the carpet? Yes, now you can get very good information, because this is what he deals with on a daily basis.

We're talking about relevance and authority. Basically, if your company receives a recommendation or more from someone very good and well-known in a field, visibility and sales start to increase.

Well, I know, right now it's impossible for you to start off-page analysis. The site is still in its infancy, so you don't have external links to direct users to your site's pages. However, I will show you what are the elements to analyze off-page in an SEO audit because they will be useful to you in the future, as you grow as a business.

Basically, off-page means backlinks and their nature and how they influence your authority in front of search engine bots.

The higher the number of unique domains pointing to your website pages, the better your backlink profile is. In other words, 100 links from 100 unique domains look better to Google than 100 links from a single domain.

Of course, the relevance to your niche, the authority and credibility of the respective domains and if they are high-level / TLD (if your domain extension is .ro, it is logical for Google to receive links from .ro as well, in most of it).

Although part of the link juice / trust is lost to backlinks with the nofollow attribute, their presence in a small proportion is necessary otherwise Google will consider that you have bought all the backlinks - you are liable to be penalized.

Be careful to attract links to all pages of your site, as deep as possible, not just to the first page of the site. Keep this in mind especially when buying the links yourself - let's face it, everyone is doing this because you need time to build the reputation you need for natural backlinks. Even if you use this gray SEO technique, do it with great care.

Also related to backlinks, pay attention to anchor texts. Avoid fixed anchors on exact keywords and focus instead on mentioning the brand name or long tail (broad match) keywords.

Right now, before launch, it follows all the elements we discussed in the competition chapter. See what their link profile looks like, whether or not they've been penalized, who their top partners are and learn from them, do things differently.

Use tools like cognitiveSEO, Ahrefs, Majestic, MOZ, etc. and centralize the data obtained. Keep the data at hand and build your own link building strategy based on it.

Also related to brand mentions and visibility, it is vital to have a connection between your website and Social Media pages. We will discuss more details about the elements you need in the next chapter.

Are you more interested in SEO? Great, come to the eCommerce Academy and take the SEO course: 100% more traffic and sales from Google. I can tell you for sure, from this you will learn about everything you need to do SEO for your online store, blog or presentation site.

SOCIAL MEDIA OR HOW TO TELL YOUR CUSTOMERS YOU EXIST

By nature, we humans need to socialize. From the old stories around the fire in the caves, to living in tribes, between the walls of a fortress, in a village, city, etc., people socialize. They talk about common things and interests.

To date, Facebook has managed to unite more than 2 billion users worldwide. They can in turn form communities or be part of them.

THE ROLE OF SOCIAL MEDIA

You know that saying, if you're not on Facebook, you don't exist? Well, in the case of online businesses, it's perfectly true.

Social Media is like planting a tree: it takes patience, perseverance and constant care so that, at some point in time, the first fruits of your tree appear. What you gain from your online presence - traffic, brand recognition, leads, credibility - goes further into the macro-conversion every store owner is aiming for. The sale.

We've said it before: social media isn't always the place to sell. People come here with a different emotional state, not necessarily ready to take the card out of their wallet and pay for your products but wanting to relax, have fun, brag or whatever.

The (organic) Social Media marketing strategy of any online store, including yours, should focus on developing and maintaining a healthy community around the brand - a community that tells more about you and determines repeat sales. Basically, it should take the place of word-of-mouth, person-to-person, as the most effective type of advertising you could have.

The truth is that you have a lot to choose from: you have Facebook, Instagram, YouTube, Twitter, LinkedIn, Snapchat, Pinterest, TikTok and many others. But the strategy of choosing the most suitable social network(s) depends on the specifics of the business and the behavior of the target audience.

Without wasting any more time, let's break the ice directly with how to develop the best Social Media marketing strategy for your online store.

How to choose the best channel?

The first thing - the audience. Since you don't yet have the data to create a customer avatar, your only option is to outline a minimal fictional template with the data you assume about future customers. Think about what age range they might fall into, but be careful, don't lie to yourself that you're targeting all people between 18 and 65. Even if you do, segment them into consumer groups and target them with different materials.

Then think about other demographic characteristics such as gender, marital status, whether they have children or not, geographic location, etc.

Imagine what interests your future customers might have, implicitly the audience on social media. Try to match the specifics of your business with the interests of your customers: for example, target travelers if you want to launch an online travel agency, or those interested in vegan food if you sell natural, organic soaps.

Due to the fact that people's interests are public on Facebook and other networks, here you have fantastic opportunities to reach exactly the right people who are interested in your type of product and who also have the opportunity to buy.

Once you've determined what your target audience looks like, think about what networks they frequent. In Romania, the Facebook page and possibly Instagram is mandatory for an online business. On a national level, Facebook is the network with the most users, and the presence of your brand here inspires credibility and a percentage of safety that it is real and active, not just smoke and mirrors.

The choice of one channel or several, additional, depends. It depends on the possibilities you have to be constantly active on them and if they match the specifics of the business. Not really into product videos? Then don't create a YouTube channel just to be there, but if you manage to make some videos, promote them on

Facebook. Is your target audience new to Twitter? Then don't make a Twitter page for yourself, but focus on the other channels frequented by your audience.

If you expect me to recommend setting business goals now, I prefer to refrain. You see, you can use different campaigns on social media for different goals, but the main purpose of creating a page is to build a loyal community.

Whether you want to sell, drive traffic, increase traffic, convert, or simply make sure you have an audience receptive to your messages, there are tons of specific posts you can make for each goal.

It is as clear as possible, on social networks you primarily socialize, you show that you are open and transparent, but you will also be able to make sales - I will tell you how later.

You can study social networks a little, after which you can play or test them. It is extremely important to understand their role, place in the funnel and the impact on your business. Then you learn how to use them together, so you have the chance to gain more visibility in the eyes of customers.

Your Facebook Business Page

After you understand your audience and choose your social media channels, it's time to move on to the actual creation of the pages. I will only detail here the good practices for creating and optimizing a Facebook page.

Creating a Facebook business page does not take you more than a few seconds, but it is important to choose the type of page carefully (for example, if you have a local business, create a page for this type of business from the start). For the page name, stick to your brand name, plain and simple. If it's a name that doesn't describe what you're selling, you can add a descriptive keyword here.

Linked to your page URL, after 25 likes, change it using your page name / brand name. This can only be set once, so choose it well.

CONTENT TYPE ON FACEBOOK

Use the company logo as a profile picture. During special seasons, holidays, Black Friday and the like, you can update your logo with specific elements (black background, Santa hat, etc.).

Don't forget the cover image - after all, it's the first thing displayed at the top of the screen. Use brand-specific colors and convey your unique value proposition. You can use the store's tagline and also update the image throughout the year to announce new campaigns. Or you can use a video.

Another aspect to optimize is the "about us" section of the page. Imagine that people arrive on the page, see what products you sell and are interested, then go to about and want to know details such as hours, location or web address of the site. Do you really want them to turn detective to find your contact details and business details?

The about us page should include a brief description of the store, including keywords, the address and location of the store / office (and on the map), links to the site and other pages important to you, additional information, etc.

You must have seen on other pages by now additional tabs in the menu, in addition to the standard tabs. You too can have personalized tabs to draw attention to the latest offers and news, a landing page, an event or whatever you want.

Last but not least, think about the call-to-action phrase displayed. If you have a standard online store, this can be "buy now", but if you want the user to ask you for a personalized offer, allow them to contact you directly from the button. See the other options and choose according to the needs of your business.

Basically, these were the elements to optimize on a standard Facebook page, but believe me, you only went through the easiest. Next comes the content part, the posting strategy and interaction with the audience, at which point things get out of your control.

Do you know how to treat content published on Facebook? Like cooking - for a cat-in-the-queue meal you use fresh ingredients (content), which you present on a variety of plates (different types of posts), keep things stupid-simple, experiment and cook everything with a splash of love (emotional persuasion).

In principle, your posts should be 80% non-commercial, short, addressed in the second person singular, in a friendly and natural tone, and grammatically correct. Forget corporate style or standard PR texts - they have no place on Facebook.

Try to entertain your fans and drive interaction: post pictures and videos, fun facts, blog articles, behind-the-scenes pictures and stories about the team and how your store works, make live videos, play with fans asking them questions, running short contests, answering questions, pinning the most important messages to the top of the page and providing support for those who have questions or problems.

My advice is to make a calendar for at least 3 months and determine what types of posts you will make throughout this period. Don't exaggerate with the number of them in a day, but it also doesn't require you to post x times daily because, inevitably, along the way, external factors will appear that will influence the strategy.

Also, there are a few things I recommend you avoid on your Facebook page: Don't link to sensitive topics like race, religious preferences, etc., because it might backfire faster than you think.

Avoid aggressiveness in posts (buy now, click here, etc.), redistribute old posts at a lower frequency, do not hide comments or give the impression that you are desperate for comments and likes; if you want to adopt the question tactic, make sure you have someone to answer you and ask questions that are relevant to your fans.

As a general rule, be active, interact with people and reply quickly on chat. This behavior will be publicly visible, by displaying the label "reply very quickly to messages". Therefore, other potential customers will also be encouraged to write to you, with the certainty that they are heard, not speaking alone.

And because we were talking about chat, we recently have a new concept in communication, based on chatbots and artificial intelligence. Basically, chatbots interact with your users automatically, using AI or a sequence of predefined rules to give personalized answers based on the questions asked.

Facebook Messenger chatbots are available on Facebook - they help you receive data, improve the user experience and strengthen the relationship with them.

To activate a chatbot you don't have to create it yourself. There are dedicated apps like Manychat. Pay attention, however, to the rules that appeared after the application of the GDPR.

Oh, you know what I forgot to tell you? With Facebook it's like being a mother or father. Just when you think you've put an end to it, they change the rules. In other words, you have to march on diversity and additional tricks to reach the audience. You can even turn to influencers to expand your audience, to reach an audience similar to yours.

If before you had chances for organic reach, today friends' posts are prioritized in the News Feed, to the detriment of business posts, by default, your posts. As long as you don't boast tens of thousands of fans or more (even then), you need to promote your posts and also use paid advertising tools. Within Facebook you have Facebook Ads, but we will discuss this topic a little later.

Don't forget to analyze your social media strategy either; use Facebook Insights and the other analytics programs available on the channels used and observe the behavioral pattern of the fans, the evolution of the page and customers. Based on this data, you will adjust your Social Media marketing strategy because you certainly don't want to find yourself investing and talking to yourself in the desert.

Do you remember that I was talking about the importance of social networks in the SEO chapter? To make the connection between the site and the social pages, implement like and share buttons, including in the company blog.

PPC CAMPAIGNS FOR YOUR ONLINE STORE

It's Monday morning, 7:20. From 9:00 you have a very important meeting, but at 8:00 you have to drop the children off at school.

Tell me, do you choose to prepare a romantic bath, with foam and scented candles, or do you take a quick shower?

This is what PPC campaigns are all about. When you want to speed things up, you need actions to help you, and you can't afford to wait.

An old saying tells us that you need to invest money in order to make money. You've probably heard it a million times too. But is this expression still valid, even today?

Well, yes, you need a budget to start a business and make it grow faster. However, how big or small it is depends on a lot of factors.

So why the big deal when it comes to paid advertising? The standard definition of advertising clearly tells us that it deals with the promotion of goods, services, people, institutions, ideas, etc., mostly through paid messages.

Obviously, we all look for the least expensive channels of promotion, but here there is a high probability of falling into a vicious circle. If it's cheap, it doesn't necessarily mean it's good. If it's good and cheap for the online store, it doesn't mean it's as good for the customer. And if it's cheap, it's not fast either.

Paid advertising tools such as Google Ads or Facebook Ads cover exactly these needs.

Also here we can even include affiliate campaigns, based on performance: a set cost only for the set conversion.

PPC campaigns bring results much faster than SEO or Social Media strategy. In this case, when preparing the launch campaign, you don't even need a customer base or an audience that already knows you. You can reach this artificially, with just as good results as if you were to reach out to existing customers.

Denying the impact of PPC campaigns or prohibiting yourself from using them on the grounds that they are expensive is the equivalent of strategically placing a stick in the wheel. I mean, a very bad decision, from my point of view.

You see, before you know the type of possible campaigns and the resources needed for each individual case, it's easy to overestimate the costs. But let's not talk about PPC budgets now, let's start with the basics.

PPC with Google Ads

To create and optimize a PPC campaign with Google Ads, of course, you need an account. Creating a new account can take less than 10 minutes and consists of 3 steps.

You log in with your email address, set the address of the site you want to promote, set the first campaign, set the payment and invoicing dates and that's it. Please, almost done. To get off to a good start you need to have Google Analytics code implemented (also link your Ads account to Analytics), Google Ads conversion code and remarketing lists - and make sure they've been implemented correctly.

With Google Ads you have two main channels where you can present yourself: Search and the Google partner network (including YouTube, Gmail, etc.). Depending on the campaign objective, you choose the right channel, promotion type, keywords, time slot, extensions, ad group and audiences.

Decide why you want to run a PPC campaign. Do you want to sell? Do you want to attract leads / contact details of people interested in what you sell? Do you want to increase the number of participants at an event such as the launch of the store? From the objective you can move on to choosing the desired channel and type of campaign.

In principle, you can create campaigns on Search (only on search or with extension also in Display) - campaigns suitable for most online stores, which are triggered when searching for certain keywords, campaigns on Display (for which you need creative and relevant banners , so focus on the visual), shopping campaigns (Shopping Ads), video campaigns on YouTube (also suitable for creative approaches) and Remarketing campaigns, targeting those who have entered your website at least once (can be carried out both on search as well as on Display).

Next comes the creation of ad groups and setting keywords. For a start-up campaign, say, on search, determine the product or products with the most sales. Do this especially if you have a tight budget - focus on an anchor product with an ok profit margin, with public trust, a good business proposition. This way you amplify the results and invest your budget intelligently.

Choose the keywords in accordance with the name of the products plus an action phrase, if possible, and eliminate the negative keywords (key term + second hand, free, olx, emag, etc.). Don't be fooled by the idea that maybe the person clicks and is so impressed by what they find that they buy from you.

The process continues with creating ads for each keyword. What is vital here is to group them separately. Ideally, an ad group should be limited to a maximum of 20-30 keywords.

If in SEO we have performance indicators, in Google Ads you come across a diagnostic tool called the quality score. It works like the light that lights up in the car, if there is a problem. A high quality score places you higher in search and lowers your cost per click.

To predict the performance of a campaign pay attention to the quality score, improve it if it is low, and to the click rate of the keyword used. The higher they are, the more likely you are to get results.

Just one tip for improving your search ads, including your quality score: use the extensions that Google provides - sitelinks, location, call extensions, reviews, additional information, etc. Sometimes they highlight your ads on the results page and present additional, relevant information to the user.

Next, you need to make some settings to increase the performance of the campaign: choose the audience, the location of the users, the display time slot, the cost per click, the bidding options, the campaign budget and the preferred display device.

But be careful, don't make the mistakes we saw with the agency's clients. Do not select all the opportunities given by Ads (to add various extensions, increase the bid for more impressions, etc.).

A client ok'd the suggestion to add new keywords in certain groups so dozens of irrelevant words were added which destroyed the CTR and quality score.
Unsurprisingly, the traffic to the site did not convert at all.

During and after the running of your campaign it is vital to monitor and measure its data. Only then will you realize what the real performance of your strategy is and adjust it so that you grow more, while reducing costs.

PPC with Facebook Ads

Do you know why you should use Facebook Ads? Because you have no counterarguments when you see the results. Everyone still uses them, because, in the right context, they bring you extraordinary results.

Yeah, I know, I've said it before that people don't come online ready to buy, but somehow paid ads on Facebook are smarter than the rest. First of all, you should know that these ads, by their very nature, disrupt the browsing experience of users. The creativity you have and the experience you are about to accumulate will help you make ads that attract attention, make users reach you, not ignore them and continue browsing.

In addition, if the behavioral model when searching on Google urges the sensation of clicking on the first result, on Facebook the ads adapt (or should, it depends on what you have done) to the behavioral model in the network.

If you know how to do things right, you can turn Facebook ads into a continuous loop that supports both your lead collection and sales strategy, at as little cost as possible.

And it all starts with Business Manager and the Facebook pixel you implement on your site.

How to create a Facebook AD

The first step in the process of creating a Facebook ad is... getting the goal right. The platform provides you with objectives consistent with various phases of the sales funnel, starting from brand visibility, impact and up to traffic, interactions, lead generation, sales from the product catalog or store visits.

Don't be crazy about likes. The truth is that we do persuasive work with a lot of clients who want likes, more likes, more likes from their ad. Commandment number 11 of the Tablets of the Law: Do not grow a Facebook community by buying likes. Advertise to get conversions.

I continue with the standard steps of creating an ad because the details to select / fill in depend on the proposed objective. Next comes the audience choice and honestly, this is my favorite part.

Finding the right target audience for a Facebook ad is as satisfying as finding a pearl at the bottom of the ocean. You have the entire ocean at your disposal, billions of users worldwide, of which over 11 million and a half in Romania (January 2022), but you only have to focus on the places where you have the best chance of finding the pearl. Select only the audience segment most likely to convert.

The even better part is that Facebook provides you with all the filters you need to reach your segment: demographics, life events, interests (very detailed), connections, custom audiences, similar audiences, etc. Practically, you can target millimetrically, exactly the ideal customer of your business, without paying anything extra.

After you set the audience, it's time to determine the placements and the budget, daily or for a longer period. Basically, you will pay in a certain system, depending on the objective: CPM (per thousand impressions), CPC (per click) or CPA (per action, like, share, etc.).

TYPES OF FACEBOOK ADS AUDIENCE

You can set the cost per unit for bidding manually or automatically (allowing Facebook to change the cost dynamically). The important thing to know is that the budget, costs and minimum limits are directly proportional to the rarity of the action set - for example, if you do a Black Friday campaign, during that period a lot of other advertisers will bid alongside you... and the cost of the campaigns will grow. During quieter periods, costs are lower.

When you have a limited budget, for a much more productive campaign I recommend you avoid running ads continuously and set a schedule, including preferred times for display.

My advice is to not necessarily go after the lowest cost per click, especially since that translates into automatic targeting of the entire country, 1865 years, made into a vegetable pot. Always prioritize audience segmentation, even if it means you'll have a slightly higher cost per click.

Here my recommendation is to start the first campaign with a budget of 5-10$ / day, without editing the CPC/CPA part too much. Basically, you let the algorithm learn how to better deliver your ad to your audience.

You may have higher costs at first, but in a few days (if you don't change your ads) these costs slowly decrease.

Scaling ads is done when you have reached a minimum cost that you can invest. From that moment you can increase the budget to 20-50-100 $ / day.

Well, from here comes the interesting and creative part: the moment of making the ad itself. Best advice? Go crazy with the use of images. In general, posts and advertisements with creative, beautiful, attractive images capture users' attention faster and determine at least one action. However, pay attention to the text part of the image, it must not exceed 20% of the volume.

A general rule is to focus on clarity and simplicity. Don't try to convey more news in one ad, but keep the elements to a unified message, starting from the title (25 characters), text (maximum 90 characters) and the choice of the call-to-action button.

Want some "secrets" and best practices? March on emotional persuasion:
- color psychology (tests several advertising variants, with a variety of colors);

- a natural language, in a conversational tone;
- strong words ("for you", "free", "now");
- FOMO texts - urgency of action and limitation of options - "don't lose", "once in a lifetime", "last pieces" etc.);
- emotional approaches (based on fear, pride, love, rewarding immediately etc.), depending on what matches with your business or campaign.

Also choose the ad format (single image, carousel, montage, etc.) and if applicable, direct people to the best address. Choose the link well, don't necessarily walk them to the first page of your website, but to the most suitable one for your objective.

I forgot something? Yes, retarget users who visited your site but didn't buy or abandoned their shopping carts with Facebook ads. Remember to always set ad performance tracking per pixel.

Continuously monitor campaign results in Business Manager and, likewise, adjust future campaigns based on the real numbers and data you have available.

AFFILIATE MARKETING - WHY YOU SHOULD PAY FOR PERFORMANCE

Indeed, to sell online you need traffic. And if you want to speed up this process, you need to turn to paid PPC campaigns. When you get to understand this phenomenon and have daily orders in the store, you start to scale the campaigns. You increase the budget where you see it is more profitable.

The increase in the number of orders also means maturing in business, something that allows you to try new marketing actions. Such as affiliation.

Through this system, you, as an online store owner, give a percentage of the sale to the affiliate / affiliates who send users who buy your products to your site.

HOW DOES AFFILIATION WORK?

Affiliates are people who have networks of websites, blogs, social media communities or lists of email addresses and can send traffic to your website, can help you promote products, and they receive a commission only from the sales generated .

Basically, here you pay for performance, only for results. See why this is such a popular strategy? You only pay for the sales you generate - not the traffic you send.

Taking it upon yourself to create an affiliate system just for your store... would be one of the worst ideas since Napoleon's campaign in Russia.

There are systems that facilitate these services, one of them being 2Performant.com. You can test, collaborate with experienced people that you can easily find, in one place, without investing a huge budget in creating a unique system - for you - but that may not even work.

Today, the cool part is that there are already active communities around this marketing system, and you can easily interact with both affiliates and other online store owners.

In good cases, through affiliation you can generate up to 20% of sales. So you can't rely entirely on this marketing channel, and I don't recommend starting an online store with the thought that once opened, you start the affiliation and pay only for performance. That's not how things work.

Affiliates can help you reach a wider audience across multiple channels and increase your sales. But you have to understand that they won't do all the marketing for your store.

CHECKLIST FOR PRODUCTIVE COLLABORATION WITH AFFILIATES

- I can NOT display the contact and support information on all pages so that the potential customers who came through the affiliate place the order on the site and the affiliates take the commission.
- I avoid placing external links on product pages.
- If the client contacts me (if I do affiliate marketing) I direct them to order on the website.

- My product pages are complete and optimized: clear call-to-action button, descriptions, multiple product images of the same size (including in the description), clear information about variables such as size, color, stock, etc.
- Navigating my site is easy and the categories easy to understand (I don't have more than 5-7 categories lined up in the menu).
- Every page in my website has my brand symbols: the same colors, background and logo. d
- I display evidence of trust on the site, especially in the product pages, starting from testimonials, ratings and up to trust certificates, guarantees, etc.
- The order completion page is secure, loads quickly, contains no distracting elements and highlights shipping costs / free shipping.
- I have product categories for which I can offer my affiliates a higher commission than the competition.
- I can offer commission to affiliates both for selling and for email subscription.
- I can quickly answer affiliates' questions about my products.
- If I have affiliates, I clearly convey to them the products for which I receive the commission and those to which it does not apply.
- If I have affiliates and I'm part of an industry where the number of returns is very high, I have a well-established policy in terms of giving commission.
- I can offer affiliates banners and useful materials for promotion.

- I have a well-known brand in the market, affiliates can promote us with full confidence.
- I produce enough content that affiliates can use to promote my products.
- The policy regarding the confidentiality of personal data is well highlighted in my website: who has access to this data, if and to whom it is shared, etc.
- I have a page that explains the details regarding the return policy and I highlight it on the product pages.
- The product delivery information page is also complete, it includes all the details customers need to know in terms of costs or benefits.

LEAD GENERATION - HOW TO ATTRACT THE CUSTOMER

Because people only buy when they trust your brand, remember that before they give you their money and love, they need to give you their time.

The first step in this customer relationship happens when they give you their email address in exchange for something of value to them.

Ok, if so far we've talked about marketing tactics that get you in front of your target audience - they bring traffic - it's time to somehow concretize each action. In other words, let's go to a warmer area of marketing -

turning simple visitors into leads and from there into full-time customers.

But what is the lead? Basically, it's about the person interested in your products / services. And lead generation represents the process by which you collect data about the person in question, in order to start laying the foundations for a much closer communication relationship.

The lead generation strategy covers the first stages of your sales funnel, the recognition and prospecting stage or, according to the AIDA model, the attention and interest stages. See why you need this strategy?

You cannot start approaching a consumer directly by mail with promotional messages and sales offers, without asking for their consent and without setting aside some time to get to know them. Please, you can, the technique is called cold marketing, it worked at a certain point, but not today.

Therefore, long live lead generation! In addition to the practical function of triggering a micro-conversion, the lead capture strategy requires knowing the channels through which the traffic comes and the starting point for familiarizing the prospect with your brand.

Unless you sell personalized services and a discussion on the phone would be more edifying than any other channel, the data you need from the user is the email address, the name and the first name. Well, trying to get the phone number or other data (excluding sensitive ones) is just your business. You might get them, but from the point of view of optimizing the conversion rate, it is not very advisable

Now let's see where the leads are coming from. Mainly, it's about all the strategies we've discussed so far: they come from keyword research in search engines, Social Media, but also from other sources - blog, forums, physical or online fairs and events, price comparisons, specialized sites etc.

Also, a good proportion of leads come from unknown sources or at least that you cannot count online. Maybe the prospect heard about you from a friend, maybe it comes because of contact with several marketing channels, online and offline, or who knows where else.

What I am trying to convey to you here is that you are not allowed, you are not allowed to use only one marketing channel to attract potential customers. If you want leads - and believe me, you want them - you need a multi-channel marketing mix. By doing this you gain some control over your business, you don't go around breaking the bank and praying for a miracle.

The standard ingredients of the on-site lead generation strategy are the lead magnet, the optimized landing page, the data capture form and the call to action. Basically, whether you want to sell them products or give them something free / discounted to get their email address, you need all of these elements.

The lead magnet is the very element that attracts attention and motivates action. So choose a useful and relevant magnet for the user, otherwise you are presenting it for nothing. One of the most effective offers that won't affect your profit margin and doesn't cost too much is the guide or eBook.

In practice, you make a guide with useful information about your products (for example, if you sell gifts you can target married couples with *"10 sweet gifts for bitter mothers-in-law"* or if you sell children's products *"How to choose the safest car seat for your child "*). It doesn't have to be long, an article of 1000 words or even less is enough, which you organize as graphically as possible.

Be careful though, even if the guide is a less expensive resource for you, it is not suitable for every online business. Instead of the guide, you can offer a discount, a gift, a gift voucher or another type of benefit that attracts the type of targeted customer.

Now the question is where do you place the lead magnet? The main place is a landing page created strictly for capturing information. The advantage of a landing page is that it eliminates any element that could distract the user and, thus, favors the completion of the action in the shortest possible time.

How to build a landing page

I'll show you how to build and optimize a landing page, including the elements of the form, call-to-action button, and magnet placement.

You can use LeadPages or, if the platform provides you with native tools for creating a landing page. And from here on, we'll go step-by-step through each element that needs to be on your page.

First, remember that not everyone likes surprises. Keep the same message, graphics and colors from the traffic source (PPC ad, banner, pop-up, etc.) to the landing page. Use the same keywords, the same benefit (and the same name for that benefit), the same colors, and the same call-to-action phrase. Don't risk your creativity because you'll confuse the user and there's a good chance they'll leave.

Continuing the idea, don't place product ads or additional offers on the landing page because you're giving them alternative channels they could choose from instead of filling out the form on the landing page. Possibly keep the additional offers for the thank you page, displayed after you have received the lead's data.

People browse a web page differently than they read a book. Your landing page is not Harry Potter and the Philosopher's Stone. So make sure that when people scan your page, they quickly find the essential information highlighted and the content is easy to consume.

What an optimized landing page should include: a clear title, subtitle, description of the offer with an emphasis on benefits, suggestive images / an explanatory video and elements of trust (testimonials, guarantees, credibility marks, etc.).

Regarding the form with which you actually capture the data, remember what I told you about the checkout form: be concise, minimize as much as possible the number of fields to fill in and clearly mark the mandatory versus the optional ones . Avoid captchas and don't tell the user that *"we don't do spam"* - avoid the word spam.

The action button must keep the same color as the one in the traffic source, without imperative verbs that leave no room for choice for the user. You can use strong words, for immediate action - "now", "today", "want", 1st or 2nd person singular, etc.

With this button tell people what happens when they click. Are they going to get a guide? Do I get a discount? Add a product to cart? Make it clear that this will happen, don't limit yourself to "send", "submit" or other deadpan words.

By optimizing the landing page in this way, you shoot the proverbial rabbits with a fire: you get the micro-conversion and lower the bounce rate on the site, which, remember, is a positive signal for Google.

How can you still capture leads? You use the popups intelligently, both those for subscribing to the news and those for the intention to leave the page, questionnaires, hello bar or floating bar (at the bottom / top of the page), you use push notifications, you create a lot of relevant content on blog and site or you can guest post on other sites, where you make sure to mention in your signature the links to your Social Media pages, your website or a favorite landing page and the rest of your contact details.

In lead generation, as in your entire marketing mix, creativity is the limit. Do not forget the offline means of attracting leads: events, business cards, stickers, gift cards for the client's friends, videos when unpacking the product, co-marketing through partners, etc.

My advice and the best I can give you is to automate the entire capture process. Use marketing automation and specialized tools such as pop-up modules, OptinMonster, Active Campaign, MailChimp and so on. Take a look at the eCommerce Academy or do a search for lead generation tools, you'll find them right away.

Don't forget the GDPR either: make sure that the lead has given you clear and explicit consent that you can process their data by ticking the consent box.

EMAIL MARKETING - LOVE YOUR CUSTOMERS LIKE YOUR SPOUSE

We are talking about one of the first digital communication channels, which originated in 1971, when Ray Tomlinson developed this system to send messages between computers.

Even if new communication channels appear such as direct messaging on chat, which is used daily by millions of users with Facebook Messenger, WhatsApp or many others, email still generates the most sales when we talk about the performance of marketing campaigns

I repeat: people buy when they trust your brand. And that is earned over time.

Do you know the expression, ``*the money is in the mailing list*"?

Well, here's a big problem. Because people won't start buying, giving you money, just because they gave you their email address or phone number.

The leads won with such care must be nurtured, warmed up, guided step by step to the sale. This process is a new strategy in its own right, which your online store also needs. Generally speaking, we are talking about the email marketing strategy here.

I receive more than 50 emails and I try to read all the important ones (about 20-30). Think of it as exactly the same for your lead, except he doesn't have the same interest in going through all the emails. But this can be changed. With a well-designed program you can train your leads to wait for each new email, to open it and ideally to buy once, twice, three times and so on.

Because the email marketing strategy is not limited to how the mail looks or how often you send newsletters. Oh, I get a lot of questions about what to look like, what products to promote, and the like, but almost no entrepreneur I talk to has a lead/customer onboarding program implemented in their business. And here many benefits are lost.

The main ingredients of the email marketing strategy are the captured address base, segmentation, the emails themselves, organized from objective to legal aspects and monitoring the results. These ingredients represent the standard steps you need to go through to make sure you get what you set out to do from the start.

But first let's see what types of emails you can and should send to your base. The need to use them is triggered by certain consumer behaviors or actions. Thus, when subscribing, it is advisable to send a welcome email that starts the onboarding process, presents the business and the main benefits / differentiating elements and indicates the next step.

Then, functionally, you need order confirmation emails, stock notification or return of the product in stock, password recovery and email when registering a new account in the store.

Depending on the lead's behavior, send abandoned cart recovery and reminder emails. And for marketing and sales, you need emails after the customer receives the order, on the customer's anniversary, newsletter, review requests and others.

Before we talk about what your email should look like, there are some legal and ethical issues to discuss. And I start with the bad habits - sending unsolicited commercial emails. Although I mentioned this in the previous chapter, it is never suggested that you buy a database of email addresses, to which you can send mass emails.

The people behind those addresses don't know you, they don't know who you are and what you do, maybe a percentage of them aren't even valid, people will ignore your messages, unsubscribe, or worst case, complain instead right, and this is where the madness begins.

On the other side of the coin, how do you know you've got the lead's consent? The man willingly gives you his address, accepts the terms and conditions, ticks the newsletter subscription box and the consent box, etc.

That's why, before you set out to send your first email, you need the lead generation strategy presented earlier.

From a legal point of view, each email must include your identity or that of the sender of the message (your store, an employee, etc.), a valid address to which the user can reply, and the visible and free option to unsubscribe.

Tips & tricks for building emails

And now let's move on to what interests you, the construction of the email itself. Depending on the objective you have set for yourself (to increase sales, educate the lead, drive more traffic to the store, shorten the sales cycle, build consumer loyalty, etc.) and the type of email, it has a different structure. However, the standard elements are the subject or title of the email, the design, the content and the message conveyed. The vital element of all is... the subject.

The subject or title of the email is practically the trigger of the action. If it highlights you, is compelling and grabs the recipient's attention, then the message is open and you are somewhere 50% closer to the goal.

Give yourself the most time to create and select the right topic. Make several variations, short, describe what the person is going to find in the body of the email, use techniques such as urgency of action, strong non-commercial words, questions, etc. You can even test the submission with two different topics and see exactly which one performs and which one is worth trashing.

Once the topic has been chosen, it's time to determine the design of the email. Always watch out for mobile users, over half of the audience opens their messages on their phone. So go for responsive and a simple, minimalist design, without too much clutter or clashing colors.

To graphically support the message sent, use images, gifs or videos, but be careful, sometimes the images don't say a thousand words, especially if they don't open automatically when accessing the email. Always optimize them with Alt-text and offer the possibility to view the mail in the browser, fully loaded.

Highlight the most important information by placing it at the top of the screen and segment the text; use white spaces, dots, lines, etc. so that the recipient can easily scan and understand the essential points.

Also, don't go too long with the text - people don't feel like reading novels at 7 in the morning, while drinking their coffee, at one o'clock, during their lunch break, or in the evening when they arrive tired from work. If you still have more to say, direct them to the site via a link. From there they are more likely to reach the end point (purchase or other conversion).

Personalize the email with the store logo, use colors representative of your brand and try to get a reaction from the customer. Even if he doesn't enter the site, ask him a question, ask him for his opinion, ask him for a review, whatever, at least get an answer.

Pay attention also to the signature in the email. Help the customer remember who you are and what you do, tell them your name, contact details and how to get to your Social Media pages or website. Personalize each message by speaking in the second person singular and, if you know, address them by name.

The content and subject of your mails depend extremely much on the recipient, because it is not recommended (nor efficient) to send the same content to all your address base. First, you need to segment it.

About segmenting your database

Without a teasing campaign, without a launch strategy, etc., it's time to bring the world into the store to generate sales.

The first thing is to send a newsletter with super offers to all the customers who until then bought the products from the offline store. So to existing customers.

Too many businesses still operate on the "hit and run" or "hit and pray" principle, hoping that at least some of the recipients will respond favorably. This principle is not a strategy. And today, when you have so many tools at your disposal, it's a shame to perpetuate the mistake.

The segmentation process is as complex a strategy as you want it to be. Generally speaking, there are 3 types of segmentation: tactical, strategic and situational. How you do it depends on the data you have about the customer and which you are constantly tracking to identify new opportunities.

Segmenting your base goes hand in hand with adding addresses at various stages of your sales funnel.

And this is where the fun really begins. In principle, you can divide the base into 3 stages.

In stage 1 you have interested consumers. They've given you their email address for a coupon, guide, etc., but haven't bought anything yet. Your goal, therefore, is to incentivize their first purchase, ideally by immediately sending an email with the exact offer they signed up for.

In stage 2, you have captivated consumers, those who have bought one or more products. Your goal is to drive them to buy again, and again, and so on.

In stage 3, you have the people who have stopped buying and even opening your emails. Your goal is to reactivate them, get them to open emails, click on links and eventually buy again.

How do you know what stage each address in your database is in? Simple, you look at the numbers again and create various avatars that you associate with each individual group of addresses. For these, you determine the demographic characteristics, location, interests, behavioral patterns and track the actions on the site, the sources they came from, etc., to do real-time segmentation as well.

Have you read an article about Google Ads and subscribed to download the guide? Then we will send you mostly articles and offers for PPC strategy with Google Ads. In addition to the fact that these emails are more effective, it is common sense to send the lead what he wants, demonstrated by his actions, not to take it for granted.

The other side of the coin is a little darker. If the man bought a phone or a watch or a refrigerator from your store, don't go on the principle that he is an obsessive buyer of phones, watches or refrigerators. No, he certainly does not want to change his phone, watch or refrigerator on the second, third day, for something better.

Using automations, better send him complementary products: accessories for the phone he bought (I don't know, an external battery, a case, headphones, etc.), watch accessories (straps, bracelets, batteries, storage box, etc.) or other household appliances to change the look in the kitchen (a microwave oven, a stove, a washing machine, a food processor, etc.). See what products they are looking at and target the user exactly with them.

Onboarding process - Familiarization with the brand

I'm still moving forward with the onboarding process, but I haven't explained how you can do it yet, have I? Well, basically, onboarding is a sequence of emails outlined from the moment of receiving the email address. It is a flexible sequence, being influenced by the actions and behavior over time of the respective user.

Let me give you an example. Let's say a user comes to your site, sees that he can receive a guide from you, is interested and gives you his email address.

Congratulations, you have obtained a new lead, a potential client has given you permission to contact him. So, you are not allowed to leave it in.

It's time to meet him and teach him who you are, what you do, what benefits he has to gain from your brand as opposed to your competitors, and what is the next step for him to take. In this phase of indoctrination, you are not allowed to sell them.

I know, it seems paradoxical since you want to sell by email, but the welcome message does not have a sales role, but that of creating an emotional connection with the potential customer. Like shaking hands and making sure you got each other's name right.

Next comes the capture phase in the sequence, where you make him personalized offers on the topics he's interested in (based on segmentation). Whether we're talking about personalized newsletters, educational emails or a sequence of warm-up blog articles followed by an offer, your goal is to captivate the user by directing them to their favorite pages on the site.

Generally, this type of sequence - educate and then pitch - gets you at least one purchase. The length of the sequence depends on the type of product and the price - at higher costs, the customer needs more time to think.

Then you have the upliftment or loyalty part, after the customer has bought at least once. The content of your messages is personalized according to the actions taken - follow up on the purchase with a review request, upsell and cross-sell, an email in which you ask the customer if everything is okay and congratulate him for the choice made, VIP coupons for loyalty etc. Through these emails, you try to make sure that the person returns to the site and buys more. In fact, this is where the real money is.

Often, it happens that you reach the stage of reactivating customers / leads. The person may have bought, maybe not, but you notice that he doesn't even open the emails anymore or maybe opens them, but doesn't click on the link. In this case, reminder emails, limited discounts on the action and re-introduction to the brand with at least one special benefit (for example, *"we are X, we miss you, come to the site and offer you x% discount until this date"*).

If you don't get a response even after the reminder email, remove the inactive subscribers from the list (and tell them clearly that you do, in a final email). Trust me, if they sit around for nothing, don't react, they will consume your resources like crazy. Beware of putting money into a base that treats you with indifference.

The type of sequence we discussed earlier works well for any type of online store. Obviously, the messages must be aligned with the brand culture and the type of offers you can make.

As for the frequency and time of sending the messages, they depend on a lot of factors. In general, emails are opened within the first 4 hours after they are sent, so think carefully about what your type of customer is doing and if they have time to read your messages during this time.

Follow the statistics in your industry (you can find them with a Google search) and, best of all, test it yourself. Create a sending calendar for a limited period of time and play with the time slots to see when the most emails are opened and when users react by clicking on the links in the message.

Constantly monitor your email marketing strategy and use automatic emailing services (MailChimp, Active Campaign, Newsman, Conectoo, GetResponse, etc.).

Why automation? Because you save a lot of resources! Plus, you react faster and ensure a good experience for today's consumer in the age of speed.

With small, snail's paces, but prompt reactions on email, in time you too will reach the top cherries/sales, exactly when they are sweetest.

BLOG - YOUR CONTINUOUS AND CHEAP SOURCE OF LEADS

How do I increase traffic to my website? How do I turn it into leads? How can I ensure that I have visibility in Google? How can I get more sales? All the answers can be found in one place: the company blog.

Blogging is one of my favorite subjects. And the good news is, it's one of Google's favorites so you need it, no question. The blog means creativity and relevance intertwined for a kaleidoscope of business objectives. From trust, to 10 experience and sales, the company blog is a conglomeration of fast and efficient little salespeople who can take you to the top - that's if you know how to do things right.

Yes, I know, it seems like I'm overstating the concept, but consistently posting content with relevant audience information, personalization, and various types of articles can get a new, inexperienced business to the top at a much lower cost than any other marketing strategy.

Right now we're talking about the technical aspects of blogging as well as some basic copywriting lessons for a business blog that's not only eye-catching but sales-boosting. Let's take them one at a time.

BLOG SALES FUNNEL

About the blog on a technical level

If until now there were worries about penalties, today the penalties are done at the page level, not on the whole domain, so if you made a mistake, sent a link to an inappropriate domain, etc., you can react individually, faster, no you wait too long to look for the source of the problem.

Keep store and blog identifiers (logo, tagline, colors, responsive design, etc.) and optimize each blog page, each new article, for search engines. You know what this means: apply the on-site and off-site optimization rules we discussed in the SEO chapter, just like you would in your online store.

When it comes to pagination of blog articles, don't pile up information like in the Bible.

Make the text as readable as possible, easy to scan using different font sizes for headings and subheadings, bullet points, bullet points, use images, videos and gifs, as well as internal links, directing readers to relevant pages on the topic. It also displays the products you're talking about for sale via the shopping buttons.

Don't forget the main purpose of a blog: capturing leads. Display a lead magnet (a guide, an eBook, etc.) and motivate people to give you their email address. You can also use popups with blog subscription forms or place them at the end of articles / in a hello bar, making sure that the user has understood the amount of value you offer and is eager for more

Use share buttons on social networks, and when promoting articles on Facebook, Twitter, LinkedIn, etc., use UTM parameters / shorten links with Bitly.

The question that remains is: what do you blog about? Well, creativity is a bottomless sack, so you have a choice.

In principle, you have a multitude of article types at your disposal:

- "how to" tutorials;
- lists;
- pro and con debates;
- case studies;
- problem / solution posts;
- article series;

- interviews;
- store updates and presentations;
- product advice and suggestions;
- trends;
- fairy tales;
- humorous articles;
- news;
- contests;
- customer generated content;
- infographics;
- podcasts; videos.

The list can go on and on, so no more lack of inspiration.

Blog copywriting ideas

Ok, one is the type of articles and another is what you actually write in them. The idea is to adjust what the market gives you to what is relevant for your consumer. You may find that he has trouble using your products, or doesn't know how to accessorize them, or doesn't know when and where to use them. You have to be the expert, the personal consultant who tells him what to do and how to do it.

When you gain the trust of the customer so that they turn to your blog every time they have a problem or concern and even tell others to consult it, you can pat yourself on the back. But not much, because you have to keep making quality content.

Now, some content related rules. The human brain is not set to think abstractly, but to think in stories. Therefore, when you choose to tell them something related to the product and add a good dose of personality, the person forgets that you are selling them something. From the way of storytelling and interpretation of the story you can convince him to make the next conversion, with finesse and subtlety.

Sales pitches are more visible than a brick in the face, and bombarded with so many sales pitches every day, any individual reacts with frustration or indifference. Give up the corporate style, clichés and jargon, because they don't work on the blog. Let me give you a concrete example of how to approach readers.

Let's say you have an online toy store. To ensure that parents - the target audience - constantly return to the blog, you create a series of story-articles in which the toys in the store are involved.

When writing, always imagine the consumer's real-time reaction. Scrolling through your phone out of boredom? Does he howl when he hears your bombastic expressions? Or is he waiting with bated breath for the sequel? Allow time for creating the articles, but especially for editing them, address yourself and count carefully how many times you say "I" or "we".

Remember that your articles should be with and about your consumer, not about you. Show them benefits, not functionality ("*Innovative office chair from a world-renowned factory*" versus "*The first office chair that doesn't hurt your back. Used by over 5,000 people*").

- place the most important information at the beginning and end of articles (people tend to ignore the middle part);

- includes strong words, emotions and sensory words (*"delicate and silky texture"*, "delicious caramel aroma", "a fine and soft material", etc.);

- provides reliable evidence; treat the community with exclusive materials (for example, give a name to the community around your brand);

- create a common enemy at which you throw stones (something impersonal - lack of time, lack of activity, lack of motivation, etc.);

- don't forget to use the content generated by the clients - testimonials, personal stories for the publication of which you obtained the consent, unboxing.

Actively promote your blog articles on Social Media pages, email (in newsletters, etc.) and on all available channels, so that you bring as much traffic that converts to your website as possible.

Monitor your blog with Google Analytics, publish regularly and update your old content. Over time, the blog will prove to be an invaluable marketing channel.

VIDEO MARKETING WITHOUT SHENANIGANS

Yes, more and more video content is being consumed. Internet speed and device performance allow us to do this, at every moment of the day and in almost every location.

If a picture is worth 1000 words, a clear video helps even more.

From cat videos, to comedy videos, how-to tutorials, to tutorials and motivational messages, we humans are spending more and more time consuming videos.

Now the idea is to make the content that your audience wants to see.

Here everything starts from market research actions. And you can do this very simply, starting from the analysis of the questions from customers, from the phone conversations you have or chat discussions.

You can go further with the analysis of discussions in Facebook groups. See where what questions are - and especially what answers.

You can also analyze the keywords used in Google searches. Identify their monthly search volume, if they are seasonal searches, and what results you find on the first page of the search engine.

Such analysis helps you to always have the best content, which practically provides the most relevant information to your audience.

I recommend that you periodically step out of your comfort zone to see what is happening in the world. See what trends are emerging and use them to your advantage.

The social events that happen around you on a daily basis can be your best ally if you want to do that. Or your worst enemy, if you're doing contextual marketing wrong.

Our goal is to help as many people as possible sell online. And a store's traffic and marketing campaigns are key to doing that. But when you do them strategically and well thought out, they have a bigger impact.

What conclusion do you draw from this?

Television is moving online, where you decide when and what you want to watch.

Through video marketing you can get closer to your community, users can instantly interact with the content posted by your brand, everything becomes more transparent and your trust in front of them increases.

And how do you do video marketing? You start in reverse, from tail to head.

This is the first and most important rule in video marketing. Because the type of video, its duration, the topic, are things dictated by the channel you share.

People on Facebook don't always turn up the volume when watching videos. And on YouTube, people prefer longer videos - which appear even higher in search. But on Instagram you can't upload videos longer than 1 minute.

Before you start filming, think about the habits and behavior of the people you are targeting.

The second most important rule is to create videos with the goal of using them in multiple places, channels, forms in mind.

You see, there are two parts to the process of creating a strong online presence.

The first relates to the entire field of content that you prepare to get visitors to the site: blog articles, Social Media posts, advertisements, emails.

And the second is about, well...

No matter how big of a presence you've managed to create, you'll need to convert traffic and visitors into customers and conversions.

Because, at the end of the day, it's not the traffic that pays your bills and fills your bank account. Sales and customers do.

And this is where video materials and video marketing can help you.

Create a YouTube channel

We are talking about the second search engine in the world, which is owned by the giant Google.

It's safer that people - your future customers - search for information on YouTube by brand name, not by your personal name.

And if you still make your YouTube channel, don't forget to optimize it - use the checklist at the end of the chapter.

Once you create and optimize your YouTube channel, don't abandon it. Post constantly, including Facebook Live videos, event footage, or any other video footage you have.

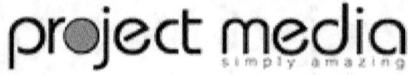

Analyzing what happens here as well, the searches made by users, the videos watched, the comments, the average time spent on a certain type of content, we realized that users and customers "migrate" between your communication channels / social networks.

Basically, those who are really interested in a certain topic, look to multiple sources of information for validation.

I can confirm that YouTube helps us acquire customers, even if only educational content is posted, nothing commercial.

The fact that for us it is well integrated in the marketing strategy, being positioned high in the funnel and that we run different PPC campaigns through Google Ads, is the subject of another discussion.

Here it is important to be discovered by your potential customers, and for them to trust your brand.

Post your videos on Facebook

It is advisable to upload videos natively to Facebook because they are 10x more shared on the network than YouTube videos (according to Quintly). They have autoplay with or without sound, which is a little misleading when you look at the metrics.

But overcoming this drawback, the fact that it runs automatically increases your chances of capturing people's attention.

I recommend using short videos with subtitles (if the sound isn't on) and putting your best effort into the first 2-4 seconds - if you show them something interesting from the start, they'll stop scrolling.

Don't forget the call-to-action - decide if you just want people to share your video or if you want to attract them to your site to capture their email address or buy something.

Go live on Facebook

Live videos on Facebook are among the top types of posts with the most interaction on this channel. And you can use them regardless of the industry in which you operate.

Provided you are creative enough.

What you can live stream on Facebook?

- Introduce your team or give a tour of your office so people can see *"where the magic happens"* in the back of the shop
- Host a live Q&A session with your Facebook followers
- Film live product usage tutorials
- Present your product in detail Film experiments with your products / comparisons
- Record an interview with an expert in your niche / an influencer
- Explain the rules of a contest, to make yourself easier to understand

- Film moments from an event you have organized or are participating in

You can find topics. You will only need good light, a high-performance device (it can even be your phone, in the first phase) and make sure to announce your intention to go live in advance.

I recommend you stay live as much as possible, because in the first few minutes Facebook may not show your video in the News Feed (to avoid possible technical problems).

Note that the video left in Facebook after the live session can be downloaded and uploaded to YouTube or Instagram.

After the live session, if you had interaction and comments, you can make a blog post on this topic, where you can upload the recording to YouTube.

The idea is that you can use a piece of content for more time and on more channels / social networks.

Use video in product descriptions

The site is your own playground. So why not experiment with video too?

What kind of videos can you use? Presentation of the product from all angles, the product in use, tutorial on how to use it, comparisons with a similar product. The idea is to supplement the lack of detail in the images, to motivate the purchase.

Many of your customers are confused because they don't know what the product would look like in reality:

how big or small it is, what the colors look like, what it looks like used or worn by a real person, what the features are, how it can be used, and so on .

Now things are simpler, you can - and I recommend you do - make videos for your products with your mobile phone. It will help you enormously, it is not necessary to have cinematic quality video materials.

Customers appreciate authenticity.

Use Instagram stories

You can use video materials on Instagram in multiple ways: you can post short videos, up to one minute long, you can do live or you can confidently use stories.

How?

- Tell a story behind the curtain (how you prepare for a campaign, how the product is made, how it is used, etc.)
- Make a tutorial for how to use the product
- Promote your latest blog post with a short video
- Display a list or countdown
- Promote your limited discount campaign

- Promote a special contest or discount coupon for Insta followers
- Present news, news or updates related to your company

Don't forget to entertain or educate your followers, in the most aesthetic way possible: people are on Instagram to follow lifestyles they want, not to be the target of your commercial offers.

Even the promotional campaign for this book started from an Instagram Story post.

Encourage customers to make videos of your products

As you already know, testimonials are extremely powerful social proof, motivating the decision of undecided customers.

Video testimonials take everything to the superlative because a potential customer will realize that the statement of the satisfied customer is real, will be able to identify with him and will be motivated to want his product even more.

But you don't have to plan a head-to-head video review if you don't have the time, the necessary tools, or your client isn't willing to sit and film with you.

Invite your customers to make a video when they unbox the product, film their reaction or how they use it

and send the footage to you, upload it somewhere on your website or post it on Social Media with a hashtag.

To encourage them, you can offer them a gift voucher or a discount code for their next purchase.

Use video in the landing page

Videos increase the amount of time people stay on the page, build trust in the brand, humanize it... plus many people prefer to watch a video instead of reading a very long article.

In a landing page you should take into account trust, the pleasant experience for the user and the clear transmission of information. So if you use a video here, you can take down 3 rabbits with one shot.

Things to keep in mind when using video on a landing page:

- Test the length of the video - many people do not have the patience to watch a long video until the end, while others would like to know all the details. Test it.
- Test autoplay vs. click - autoplay is generally something people hate because it interferes with their experience. On the other hand, it can increase the conversion rate. Test to see how the situation is in your case.

- Display a call-to-action - you can display it throughout the video or at the end of it, but be sure to clearly specify to people what they have to do next.
- Use a script - this way you make sure that you have fluency and the ideas have a logical continuity throughout the duration of the video.

You can be the one presenting the product / service in the video, or it can be an advertisement-type presentation video. You could also use visual cues (a hand pointing in the direction of the call-to-action button, the protagonist's gaze directed towards it, etc.).

Use video presentation / tutorial on homepage

Ok, the front page of your website is no longer necessarily the user's first point of contact with your business. But still, it's a landing page for most people and search engines.

By using a video presentation here you can ensure that you improve the time spent on the site and attract the attention of the visitors.

I recommend creating a pitch video where you talk or present your site and team to build trust and demonstrate that there are people behind them capable of helping them with what they need.

Use video on your blog

Video used in blog posts also works as a hook to grab people's attention.

If you didn't know, the time spent on the site and the number of pages visited is a factor taken into account in SEO. The more people seem interested and stay longer, researching other pages, the higher Google will place you on the results page.

And you remember, I told you earlier that more and more people would rather watch a video than read a very long article. So combine them.

Make videos based on your articles (and vice versa) and post both on your blog. Record videos and turn them into a podcast (which you then post on your blog). Or in a PowerPoint presentation that you post on your blog and SlideShare.

That's how you give people the opportunity to choose to consume the content in the form they want for themselves. And that means a better experience for them.

Choose the videos you use carefully:
- presentations (product, team, office / warehouse tour) are suitable to attract traffic
- educational videos play a major role in capturing leads
- product comparisons, tutorials and demo videos influence the sale best.

Join TikTok too

The application launched by the Chinese became available worldwide in 2018, and the pandemic gave it a super boost of growth.

Due to the type of content posted here, especially during the market entry period, many entrepreneurs consider this channel to be less suitable for business development.

But new statistics show that the number of TikTok users in Romania exceeds that of Instagram users. So I see a great opportunity.

Social media is about socializing, it happens between people, business is done between people, and social media allows brands to interact with customers and potential customers. The idea is that your presence and activity here helps you gain the trust of a growing number of potential customers.

VIDEO MARKETING STRATEGY CHECKLIST

Youtube

Pay attention to the first 10-15 seconds of your video - you have very little time to grab people's attention so give it your best shot here. Draw, use a hook, focus on the story, but whatever you do make sure you don't bore the followers.

Use frames with human faces to convey and evoke emotion.

Change the camera angle from time to time. People get bored quickly.

Be consistent with your brand image and mission. Even if you talk about things that are apparently not related to the products you sell, convey the feeling that your brand usually conveys.

Never place important text (in fact, no text) in the lower-right of the video.

Always have a call-to-action - both written and verbal. If people like your message and are interested, guide them to where they can learn more and buy. Usually it's your website.

Always have a story or make one. Keep your eyes open to what's going on around you and talk/film situations and issues that people can relate to.

Prepare a thumbnail (again, no text on the bottom right) with a catchy, easy-to-find title with a promise (eg how to).

Add cards to key video moments (from the Video Manager) to direct people to your landing page, a survey, or other complementary videos.

Optimize your video for YouTube:
- Create 2-3 possible tiles from which you choose the winning variant.
- Add a description of at least 250 words: set the keyword

- Mention it in the first paragraph and balanced throughout the text
- Mention the call-to-action at least at the beginning and end of the description
- Add the right tags so that your video can be easily found by interested people.

Facebook

- Add a caption or descriptive text at key moments so your video gets the message across even if people aren't watching with sound
- Capture attention in the first 2-3 seconds, otherwise people will keep scrolling and you'll lose them
- Don't create long videos on Facebook, they won't have the patience to sit through to the end
- Try vertical videos

WHAT TO DO AT THE LAUNCH OF YOUR ONLINE STORE?

After all the marketing strategies we've talked about so far, it's time to put them together for a strong campaign to launch your online store. Optimize your store, or if you have a lot of products, just optimize your top 5 pages and the pages with the products you expect to sell best.

Start building articles for your company blog (which you immediately optimize), but also pages on the most appropriate social networks (in this case, Facebook and Instagram).

Before launching the actual store, create a landing page to collect email addresses and possibly pre-orders. How do you drive traffic to your landing page? You do a teasing campaign with PPC, Google Ads and Facebook Ads. Collect the email addresses of interested people and capture their interest through your email marketing strategy.

Basically, this is how you can ensure a percentage of sales and visibility before the launch. On the day / week of the launch you can boost sales with discounts or other extra benefits, for a limited time. How would you like to launch the online store?

CHECKLIST FOR ONLINE SALES FROM THE FIRST DAY OF LAUNCH

- You have displayed a coming soon landing page on the website, where you collect the email addresses of those interested in what you are about to launch.
- Offer an incentive on the landing page - a discount, gift, guide, bonus points, access to your community with special benefits, etc.

- You have prepared the discount rules for the launch ahead of time.
- You have prepared a set of banners for the site.
- You created accounts on Facebook and Instagram where you tease before the release.
- You have added Google Analytics and Google Search Console tracking codes to the store.
- You have installed the Facebook pixel
- You have integrated with your email service provider.
- You have set email templates for autoresponders (order confirmation, invoice sending, review request, account creation, password change, welcome to the store, password recovery).
- You have prepared the emails for the actual launch, to notify the subscribers.
- You have prepared a hello bar in which you announce the date on which the offers from the moment of launch end.
- You have prepared a list of the first articles that you will publish on the company blog.
- You have prepared a press kit with a press release announcing the launch, quality images, logo and bio for the store.
- You have created a video with viral potential related to your store, your products.
- You organized an email / Facebook contest to create excitement around the launch.
- After people give you their email address, you invite them to tell 2 / 3 / 5 friends in exchange for access

to the store's special community, which enjoys more benefits than regular customers (or other incentives).
- You sent some products to opinion leaders (influencers, bloggers, etc.) whom you asked to give you an objective testimonial to use on the website at the very moment of launch.
- You have made a list of potential sources of backlinks to your store (influencers, niche bloggers, specialized sites, etc.).
- You have prepared advertising sets with Facebook Ads and Google Ads to announce the launch and the offers from the moment of launch.
- You tested the command flow to discover possible errors to avoid them at the time of release.
- You've added your sitemap to Google Search Console and checked for broken links or other errors in your store.

ONLINE BUSINESS GROWTH

If before I mentioned how important it is to act quickly for the actions you are about to take, now I can tell you that the secret of success is the persistence of your actions.

This is where the difference is made between entrepreneurs who succeed in growing their businesses and those who just want to.

Yes, adaptation to the situation is also important, plus resistance to change. Technology and the large volume of information have an incredibly large impact on customers, on the way they buy, on decision-making and above all on brand loyalty.

In this book I talk about the important concepts for running an online business.

And now, let's move on.

Time passes. And as an online business owner, two things can happen to you: either you hang on, sell consistently and sometimes have sales spikes, or you flounder and go out of business.

Now, if everything goes ok, your goal is to grow your business, earn more and automate it in one way or another to get what you decided you wanted from the start - financial security, time for yourself and your passions, or anything else.

This is exactly what you are about to read.

IN THE BEGINNING IT WAS THE CUSTOMER

(AND AT THE END)

Are you now wondering if I'm getting tired of repeating "customer", "customer", "customer"? Well, no. Today we live and sell in an environment where the customer's claims, needs and behavioral patterns determine the success or failure of a business, whatever it may be.

You can imagine that your target customer group is the heart of your business. As long as it continues to beat in the body - buy from your online store - the business continues to live. And just like a real heart, the customer group will still work even if they don't buy from you; it will continue to beat the receiver - competition - even if you "donate" it forcibly.

Now that you've reached the stage where you're thinking about your store's growth strategy, with all the bells and whistles and confetti (and there's nothing wrong with thinking that), it's the right time to take a closer look at your customers and prospects.

Why? Because you need to determine in detail who they might be, what they are interested in, where they are online and what they are doing there, as well as whether they have the financial means to buy your products.

You need to target these channels to reach the customer and customize your approach to match their interests and demographic/psychological characteristics.

Customer persona

For example, let's make the ideal portrait of a guy named Jon Snow.

This is a perfect warrior who fights for justice and is respected by many. King at 20 and ruler of the North, a kingdom he has just conquered, Jon Snow is alone and lives in a castle with his sister. He's a capable horseman, an expert swordsman, and wants to be seen as honorable. He does not know the identity of his mother, something that has been bothering him for a long time. He is experienced with returning from the dead. Personal Quote *"Different roads sometimes lead to the same castle."*

You have to create exactly the same type of fictional portrait for different consumer categories:

- have a name (this will make it easier for you to customize your approach);
- a descriptive image;
- demographic data;
- the job position and its responsibilities;
- goals and tasks related to your website;
- environment (physical, mental and technological);

- a personal quote about what matters most to the individual, but is also relevant to your product.

But let's go step by step through the process of creating a customer avatar. Practically, it starts with the definition of the business objectives related to the respective consumer, asking questions, centralizing the information and only then the actual construction of the profile.

What is your goal with your ideal clients? Do you want them to buy as quickly as possible, remove all distractions from their path, to make an immediate conversion? Do you want them to ask you for a price offer for your services? Do you want them to try a service / product and do you consider the moment when you sign a contract with that customer to be a macro-conversion? Decide what your goal is so that you have a good reason for creating the avatar.

Many wish they could create their ideal customer profile without personally interacting with existing customers. But this is impossible because your job is to find out real data from real customers. The customer avatar is not based on assumptions, even if it is a fictional profile.

In addition to the behavior patterns and reactions you observe at the time of the sale, it is important to personally ask questions, using various tactics:
- attract the visitor with a discount in a pop-up, with access only if they want to complete a survey

- send emails (follow up on the sale) after the customer has received the order, the same with a questionnaire
- you give them access to a guide or other type of resource when completing the form

Two other options to collect customer data are their personal Social Media profiles and your own gold mine - Google Analytics account. Here you find a multitude of interesting data about all categories of individuals who access your site and buy.

Now, what data do you collect about your customers? It's time to put personal preferences or opinions aside and centralize data across multiple customer profiles.

What do I mean? Let's say you have a men's fashion store. You may think you're only targeting men, but you're forgetting that a large percentage of their female partners—whether married or in a relationship—are shopping for clothes for them.

First, you collect demographic data:
- gender (female thinking and buying is different from the male);
- age;
- marital status (it's a bit ineffective to promote your dresses by bride to single women when you could be targeting couples in a relationship or engaged);

- whether they have children or not (an important piece of information for many, purely business wise - stationery, toys, fashion, etc.);
- profession (generally look for a common status);
- financial situation (see how much they are willing to pay for your product);
- objectives (why they buy your products);
- education (this conditions the approach - do you know technical terms or you have to rely on testimonials and other evidence of trust);
- the factors that influence their purchase decision;
- buying habits (see if they are interested in accessories to the ordered product, offer them the complete package if that's what they want);
- as well as other data specific to your business.

Good, you know what data you need to collect. However, you still see various articles on the net telling you that client avatars don't work, they don't help you at all.

Why? Because, just like any other marketing tactic, there are a number of common mistakes to avoid.

First, avoid creating too many avatars. At first you might be so excited that you put customers into 5-10 separate groups, although one look at the data would tell you that there are common characteristics between the groups. The creation of each avatar (2-3 or more, depending on the business) begins from a common goal or from the group of the most valuable customers.

Then, it ignores irrelevant data such as the fact that one of the customers has a boutique on the corner of the street or any other insignificant nuance for marketing or sales. Yes, it's great to know all the details about the customer, but remember that the ideal profile is a conglomeration of common data applicable to a larger group of customers.

Remember when I told you that avatars aren't built on assumptions? Avoid making assumptions and scenarios about customers to fill in the blanks in your avatar. Rely only on real data, from and about the consumer. If you don't have these, wait a little longer before building your ideal profiles.

You've made your client avatars, congratulations, but your work is far from over. Put avatars to work in your marketing and sales approach: add avatars to CRM contacts, segment your brand onboarding process based on profile characteristics, use them to plan specific goals and campaigns for each profile, target similar audiences with these in PPC campaigns, reevaluate the most valuable customer categories to target them with the minimum budget, etc.

Basically, the customer avatar plays a vital role in reducing marketing costs, including cost per conversion, and allows you to chat 1-on-1 with people.

Provided you use it.

Ultimate eCommerce Masterplan - Nistor Zsolt

project media

SET OF QUESTIONS TO FIND THE CUSTOMER PERSONA

Create a questionnaire with Google Forms or any other tool and invite customers to answer you (you can offer them a discount or other gift in exchange for their answers).

1. Age
2. Gender (female, male)
3. Civil status (in a relationship, married, single, divorced)
4. Environment of origin (urban, rural)
5. Education level (last educational institution graduated, profile studied, etc.)
6. What is your field of activity? (e.g. wholesale and retail trade, transport, construction, financial intermediation, real estate transactions, etc.)
7. What industry do you work in? (e.g. IT&C, fashion, home&deco, children's items, tourism, etc.)
8. What is the size of the company you work for?
9. What is the position you hold within the company?
10. What are the activities of a typical day at the place of the work?
11. What knowledge and tools do you need at the place of the work? (e.g. time management applications, team management studies, knowledge of processing various materials, sales, etc.)
12. How you learn new information for your job

or for personal development? (e.g. I read books, blogs, various publications, attend courses, etc.)
13. What books, publications or blogs do you read?
14. What do you want to achieve personally? (e.g. more time for family, friends, travel, etc.)
15. How do you spend your free time? What are your hobbies?
16. What are the problems you encounter on a personal level?
17. What do you want to achieve professionally? (e.g. to advance in your career, earn a better salary, etc.)
18. What are the problems you encounter professionally? (e.g. dissatisfied boss / employees, fear of taking certain risks, etc.)
19. How do you prefer to interact with sellers of products or services? (email, phone, live chat, meeting, etc.)
20. Describe a recent purchase. Why did you need the product/service, how did you evaluate the process and how did you decide to buy that product/service?
21. What worries you when it comes to buying a product / service? (eg quality, price, brand, etc.)
22. How familiar are you with our company's products / services? (I have known the company for a long time, I just heard about your products / services, I already use these products / services, I am still not sure if these products / services are the best for me, etc.)
23. What would you like to get by purchasing our products / services?

CLIENT TYPES

A lot of people land in an online store. Some of them are and remain simple visitors: they search, they wander through the pages of the site, but they are not pressed by a need, nor motivated by a desire to convert. The other side is represented by prospects, those who will buy at some point in time, buy now, or at least give you an email address.

In our industry we have various ways of segmenting customers. Personally, I will limit myself to defining five main types of customer, which most stores meet. Each type of customer is established by monitoring actions taken in relation to your website, but also behavior, interests and buying habits.

Hunters

The first and everyone's favorite customer is the hunter. He comes impelled by an urgent need, and buys without wasting time. Are you wondering why you still need to prepare a strategy for him, since he is already ready to buy? Simple, your website must meet his need, offer him that pleasant experience that conditions the conversion.

Even if the "hunters" seem like ideal customers, you must know that their attention and motivation is easily distracted. Therefore, 404 errors (pages that do not exist) are a dead end for them from which they do not return to the site, and abandoned carts behind show you how much work you need to invest in optimizing the product, cart and checkout pages .

The hunter reaches the store through keyword searches in search engines, through paid channels and directly, he already knows your address. Before we talk about the strategy for welcoming and maintaining this type of customer, I would like you to see the rest of the categories so that, in the end, you can create a unified strategy that responds to all.

Repeat customer

A second type of customer is the repeat customer, the one who keeps coming back to the site, but only buys on a strong impulse. You see this in Analytics coming directly from email or PPC campaigns. It is certain that the person entered the website at least once, maybe gave you his email address, maybe even added products to the cart, but he needs repeated visits to the product pages, by categories and in the blog, to decide.

The repeat customer has this behavior because he is emotionally motivated by fear: the fear of missing out on a better price or benefit that, hypothetically, he would have discovered with just one more click. If you demonstrate your empathy and provide the impulses he needs, the caroler turns into one of your most profitable customers.

Adventurer

The third type of customer is the adventurer, a newcomer to your site. So, the newcomer can reach your site from all the channels you make available, but this does not necessarily mean something good. From the traffic source, you can rarely tell what stage they are in with the intention to buy. You need to compare their data with your ideal profiles.

The adventurer wants to be helped and entertained, so the main places they land on are the front page of the website and blog.

The Loyal Customer and the Hoarding Customer

The fourth category of customers is represented by the loyal customer, the one you manage to convince to buy more than once from your online store. In principle, loyal customers are the ones that bring you the most value because the costs to persuade them are lower than those needed to attract a new customer.

Last but not least, every online store has at least one hoarder or, in other words, discount hoarder. Even if you know people love low prices, my advice is to use marketing gimmicks to convince them, not to drop prices too much. Hoarding customers are rarely loyal (unless you can offer them discounts on the conveyor belt), and the moment you raise costs, they will go looking for discounts.

A strategy for everyone

With the 5 types of customers in front of you, it's time to see where on the site you need to optimize their experience, so that you lead them through the sales funnel and get the desired conversion.

For the hunting customer, pay maximum attention to the product page - especially at the level of product image, descriptions and techniques to urge action. If you optimized your pages as you read in the previous chapters, you shouldn't have any problems.

For the repeat customer, prices (dynamic or price comparators) matter a lot, but also personalization and relevance, especially for those who reach the site via paid channels or via email. Add strong proof of trust to all pages of your site.

The adventurous customer or newcomer should have easy ways to get to the product via the front page (link on banners to landing pages). Also, provide them with relevant and valuable content, different from that on the websites of competing companies, which you customize based on customer avatars.

In terms of the customer's need for a discount, go back to the pricing tactics I discussed in the second chapter of the book and use psychological pricing, the anchoring technique, to offer bundled products and adjacent services that complement absence of discounts.

For the loyal customer, the loyalty strategy uses rewards and a personalized approach, depending on the buying habits observed on the site, but also on his actions. Sit tight, we'll talk about the whole loyalty strategy a little later.

WHY YOU NEED TO KNOW EMOTIONAL PERSUASION

There are 3 steps by which you can persuade people to convert to your site. First, people need to trust the site. He must be credible and have authority, a good reputation.

Then people need to experience an emotional connection with the site and what you have to offer them. And three, people need to be convinced with data, facts and numbers to convert to the site.

These 3 points are equivalent to the 3 techniques of persuasion established by Aristotle more than 2000 years ago: ethos, pathos and logos. If you are not familiar with these concepts here is their definition in relation to conversions:

- ethos refers to appearing trustworthy to the consumer with an ethical approach;
- pathos means showing people that you understand their needs and behavior, with an emotional approach;
- logos means showing people that you respect their intellect, with a rational approach.

Ultimate eCommerce Masterplan - Nistor Zsolt

project media

Selling in an online store combines all these 3 concepts - the person arrives at the site, convinces himself that he can buy from you without risk, motivates his purchase emotionally (how well he will feel after using the product) and then rationally (has free shipping, has the lowest price, etc.).

You and I and your customers buy emotionally. Basically, yes, we rationalize a decision, but only after we have already made it on an emotional level. And this fact is good news for you, as a business owner.

Because you have a multitude of emotional persuasion tactics to create or stimulate the need for the product by appealing to fear, love, pride, gratitude, surprise or any other emotion that goes with the specifics of your business. Even negative emotions like sadness, anger, guilt or shame.

Beauty sells. Pleasure sells. Authority sells, and when you emotionally position yourself as a brand, people will buy more and tell others about you, implicitly causing more sales.

So how do you increase sales and website conversions using emotional persuasion?

You see, you have two options: either you stimulate existing emotions in your audience, or you create them through design, content and approach. The truth is that you rarely know the emotional state of your potential customer, the moment they enter the store.

Unless it's Valentine's Day, Christmas, Mother's Day, Black Friday, or other events that you know are emotional mixers (love, gratitude, fear of missing out, etc.), the best strategy is to create emotional approaches that change the state of the visitor.

And it all starts with the design, including colors, fonts, images and the positioning of elements on the page. You didn't think that the font used in the website affects the psyche of the visitors? Well, look he does. When choosing a font, consider the age, preferences and habits of your target audience.

In real life, when we talk face to face with a person, we have some non-verbal cues (body language, micro-expressions, tics, etc.) that signal the intention and emotional state of that person. In your website, the equivalent of non-verbal cues is typography / font.

If on the surface it seems like an insignificant element, the invisible part depends on how the words look, on readability (people trust more in an easy-to-read font), the contrast with the background, scaling, the hierarchy of information in the texts and the tone they ,,talk".

Then the colors. Remember that a stand-alone color does not trigger emotion on its own, but is influenced by cultural preferences and the context in which you display it. Yes, blue evokes serenity and red evokes excitement, but if a color doesn't support the message conveyed through text, you're using it for nothing.

Regarding the psychology of images, it evaluates the images currently used on the site. Do you think it evokes the right emotion? Does the composition direct people's eyes to the most important message? Pay attention to the facial expressions of the characters in the images, their size, color, body language and so on.

Avoid stock photos or those taken directly from suppliers and try to bring original content. Not for Google (it can't read the content of an image - yet) but for potential customers.

Storytelling and emotions

We move from the design to the most important part of the site: the content. Obviously, you need to support the messages conveyed with videos or gifs through the movement pattern of the characters and through the sound, but I want to focus here on some emotional copywriting techniques for texts.

I also talked before about the technique of stories (storytelling) and the need to emphasize the benefits gained by the client rather than the functionalities. The point is, people really don't care what you sell. Even if you know how great your product is, how best it is, your customers are only interested in what they have to gain, how they will feel better, more beautiful, more popular, more fashionable if and after buying it.

PRODUCT STORY

Furthermore, when reading a story, people are primed from the start to read it to the end. The lack of a conclusion, an action that completes the whole process leads to the appearance of anxiety and sadness - negative emotions that make them keep coming back to the site until they get the solution.

First of all, it is vital to know that there are 8 basic human desires that you can stimulate to prepare the sale. These are *the desire for survival (lust for life), the pleasure of eating and drinking (basic needs), freedom from fear, pain or danger, the desire for sexual companionship, comfortable living conditions, the desire for superiority / gain, caring and the protection of loved ones and the need for social agreement.*

It is precisely on these types of sensations that you must go. Do you pretend to sell pride and esteem (cosmetics, jewelry, fashion, etc.)? Use words that raise the customer's position: image, respect, strong, luxury, loss, merit, influence, reputation, imagine what this one will say when she sees you with the product, etc.

Are you selling safety and comfort? Use strong words like protection, trust, care, available, immediate, easy, accessible, escape, problems, etc. Are you selling based on fear? Use loss, consequence, failure, suffering, cost, wound, etc.

What is important to remember is that an emotion does not act alone. Try to evoke a combination of emotions to make the sale: fear (for a problem) and gratitude (for the solution presented), love and immediate reward, guilt and pride (goes well on fitness and sports), and so on.

Always leave the customer with a positive emotion when making the purchase decision. Even if you "attack" him emotionally based on guilt, sadness, anxiety or other negative feelings, use them only to fuel the decision process a little, but offer the hope of a positive feeling at the end.

One more thing, try repetition to sustain the emotion. Not necessarily the repetition of the same strong words, but also of their synonyms, words from the same semantic field. I think that it is precisely because of this fact that I tend to repeat certain concepts in the articles on blogs, to be 100% sure that the person understands what I want to convey to him.

Imagine what emotion the following words could create: beautiful, precious, honor, trust, tenderness, pleasure, harmony. Did it make you think of love / belonging? But despair, unhappiness, agony, helplessness, miserable? Repetition makes you think of sadness or anxiety.

Follow the same principle when creating the texts for your website. Use universally powerful words (free, because, you, etc.), but also repetition of emotional words. Before you make your content strategy, do a little research on emotion-triggering keywords and then use them in your texts.

As a general rule, imagine the possible questions on your customers' minds (yes, even the ones that seem silly to you) and provide the answers in your content. Plus, see what their objections might be (the product is too expensive, it won't work for me, I don't know if I have time, it will be difficult to use, I can buy it later, etc.). Answer these objections from the start. For example, if

the person thinks, *"hang on, I can buy it later, what a rush"*, limit his time. Displays a countdown until the end of the offer or until it can receive the product with faster / free shipping, etc.

This way you will save a lot of time and resources on the customer support side. Be as specific as possible, give real or imaginary examples, and don't be shy about using names and characters that customers can relate to. Look at Steve Jobs, Elon Musk, Walter Disney and others, we all recognize their brands, at least by hearsay. You, the employees, the mascot of the store should be in the front line of promoting your website.

It also uses consumer-generated content: unboxing videos, testimonials, social media comments, etc. And on the subject of trust, it clearly displays the credibility marks, logos and awards you've won.

Finally, I repeat, go for the benefits that the client has to gain; explain as you would to a kindergarten child why your product is better for him than the competition's products.

THE CUSTOMER JOURNEY - HOW TO WALK A THOUSAND KILOMETERS IN THE CUSTOMER'S SHOES

The customer is the best marketing specialist you can call on. Between so many options on the market and so many sales people shouting „*Choose! Choose me,*" all at once, to the consumer the options begin to look and sound the same. It's getting harder and harder to choose who to trust.

So, when making a purchase decision, the customer will either seek the advice of those around them, or gravitate towards the firms that have done the best job of gaining trust.

Brand authority, word of mouth and reputation are and will be increasingly important, implicitly a differentiator for any business owner who wants to stand out from the crowd. Because it's a thousand times easier to be heard louder than the competition when the voice of the customers makes all the noise for you.

For years, business owners have used various interpretations of the marketing funnel (consumer journey) to define and understand the different stages a customer goes through in the consumer life cycle.

The problem is that, over time, they have perpetuated several mistakes regarding this journey: they assumed that the customer journey is exact / linear, they did not understand that the human can enter through any stage, they omitted to build a map for the post phase-sale, they did not take into account the external elements that influence the entire trip and others.

A customer journey map is an illustration or diagram of all the touchpoints an individual goes through with your business. There are a lot of templates for this map, but at the core, they all include an avatar, the steps from start to finish related to the consumer experience (including touchpoints), and potential emotions.

If you have a team that takes care of your store, it is important to include them in the process of creating the map. Because each of your employees better understands one part of the journey or another, depending on the position they occupy.

For example, the designer and programmer understand the context in which the product will be seen. Copywriters and support people know the emotions and questions on the customer's mind. And salespeople understand the entire customer journey through the sales funnel. It's vital to bring them all together - or if you're running the store yourself, understand the entire customer journey, including why they're reluctant to take certain steps.

Let's say you have an online store where you sell homewares and decorations, possibly rugs. Your customer finds you in a search on the results page or through Social Media, maybe Instagram. When he buys from you, you imagine that he searched for rugs for sale on Google, clicked on the result, found what he wanted, added it to the cart and completed the order. Sounds pretty linear, doesn't it?

Well, even if you look in Analytics and see a lot of data related to touchpoints with the site, this raw data is only a tiny part of the entire journey.

When you look at the extremely simple search and purchase process on the site, for the average consumer, it might look something like this: they see an Instagram post from a friend who just got a new rug in their house and they think *"hey, I need it too"*, he searches on Google on his mobile and clicks on the result with the highest rating, opens another tab and looks for reviews about the store, goes to eat and forgets what interested him so far.

He remembers in a week that he wants a carpet and searches again - this time from the desktop, chooses the first result on Google, thinks about whether or not it's worth the money, asks his wife / husband / friends, decides to buy, adds the product to the cart and sees that he could get it at a discount with a coupon, opens another tab and searches for a coupon, goes back to the site and applies it, completes the order and subscribes to the newsletter, but doesn't like you yet Facebook, gets the carpet, is satisfied and lives happily ever after.

Well, I think you've pretty much figured out the big picture. Suddenly, the customer's interaction with your store is more complex than you imagined - there are time gaps, switching from one device to another and multiple contextual references related to your brand.

And every interaction counts. That's why you need a map of the consumer journey from impulse to purchase and loyalty.

The steps of the consumer journey

In principle, there are several common phases in customer behavior: first they are driven by a need to look for the product, then they explore and discover the existing options, they are better informed about your product, they make a decision and make the purchase, then they are loyal.

For each phase you need to identify the user's needs, objectives and expectations, contact points (processes and channels), customer experience, problem points and external elements that influence the experience, but also the need for the product.

THE PHASES OF TRANSFORMATION INTO A CLIENT

But let's see together the process of creating a map for your business, step by step. You can use the stages I was talking about before (discovery - documentation - choice - purchase - loyalty).

Step 1. First of all, define the stages of consumer behavior. Depending on the specifics of your business, they differ. For example, if you have an online travel agency, the customer goes through exploration to find inspiration - researching the best offer - booking - experience using the service - sharing the experience after using the service.

Step 2. Align the consumer's goals at each stage. Think about what he wants to achieve from each stage so that you serve him the necessary impulses to move on to the next stage or stages that are profitable for you (acquisition and loyalty).

How do you find these goals? Consult customer avatars (don't forget that you have to create maps for each avatar separately) and use qualitative research methods such as 1-on-1 interviews with the customer, with flexible tasks depending on the answers, but also analyzing requests and objections on the tickets and support chats.

Step 3. Find out the contact points (for online stores one of the most important is the product page, for a presentation site - the price or contact page). See where the consumer's journey begins on the site and see behavior and goal reports in Google Analytics.

Step 4. See if people are achieving their goals. Are there elements in the site or external that prevent them from continuing their journey? Do you have a high number of abandoned carts on your site? Watch the Google Analytics reports again and see what actions people are taking or missing and where, in relation to touchpoints.

Step 5. Organize the map in a table or other CJM / Customer Journey Mapping application (you can find them on Google). Complete the map with the stages of the journey and, for each of them, establish the objectives, the experience, the consumer's problems, the touch points and all the elements we have talked about so far.

Step 6. Prioritize the pages / touchpoints you want to optimize first. Create your optimization and A/B testing strategy and get ready for work. To work, the customer journey map along with customer avatars must be applied to your store.

It is vital to understand one thing. When you map the consumer journey, you do it from their perspective. It's critical to put assumptions and preferences aside and look strictly at what the customer is doing, data, statistics and behavioral patterns observed when interacting with your site.

Organize your entire marketing and conversion rate optimization strategy based on what the map tells you. Thus, you will improve the current consumer experience, make organizational changes, communicate better with customers and discover new optimization opportunities.

SALES FUNNEL

The new sales funnel is shaped like an hourglass. In other words, the effort you put into attracting the consumer to the site and guiding them to the sale is directly proportional to the effort you put in after they have bought, to strengthen the relationship with the customer.

Also, the funnel is much more detailed than anything you've seen so far. Before we had the stages of exploration, capture, maintenance, transaction and retention, but today things look a little different.

The first phase is brand recognition. And you can imagine what the user is thinking: *"Do I like you? Are you relevant to me? Do I want to hear more about you in the future?"*. The engagement stage is like doing a casting to select the most qualified audience.

The second phase, the educational stage, is equivalent to identifying a problem: *"Do I have a problem?"*. Basically, the goal here is to make the consumer realize that they have a situation that obviously needs a solution.

The third phase is the research stage, equivalent to the investigation of solutions (*"What solutions exist? According to what factors should I orient myself? What alternatives exist.?"*). Therefore, the goal is to repeatedly direct the consumer's attention to the solution product, communicating its benefits, differentiating elements and capabilities.

The fourth phase is the evaluation stage - choosing the product to satisfy his need (*"Does this product solve my problems? Does it fit what I need and want?"*. How do you support your product's value in the eyes of the consumer? You add to the proposition unique value, capabilities, case studies, concrete examples of how the product works, etc.

The fifth phase is justification, in which you justify the value of the product to motivate decision-making on an emotional level (*"Why do I need this product right now? Why should I choose this one and not another? How can I make my girlfriend/boyfriend / wife / husband / mother / father or any other person see that I made a good decision?"*).

In this phase, you need to show them how many times the value invested will return, differentiating elements, social proof and demonstrations of brand authority (brand mentions, link building, endorsement, etc.).

The sixth phase is exactly what you're targeting: the acquisition, the transaction, and the transition factors from lead to customer (*"How do I buy it? How difficult will it be to use it, and how quickly will my status change once I use it?"*).Acquisition is the tipping point in the funnel, the moment it turns on its head.

The closer they get to the purchase, new questions, concerns and objections appear in the consumer's mind. Be sure to address them on the product, cart and checkout page.

The seventh phase is adoption or familiarization with the brand through educational materials followed by sales proposals (*"How do I use it? When and where? How do I enjoy the value of the product as quickly as possible?"*).

When a new customer joins your base it is vital to nurture the relationship with them to bring them closer to the brand. Make sure he has a pleasant delivery and unpacking experience, provide him with guides and videos on how to use the product, as well as upsell / cross-sell options.

The eighth phase is retention, the stage where the customer must feel so satisfied that they continue to buy from you (*"Do the people at store X care that I feel good using their product? Do I see added value? Can I see myself buying from here again? Why do I love being a customer of the store?"*).

It's vital to make sure the person is happy with their choice before you send them another sales pitch. After he has bought, ask him how satisfied he is with the purchase made, what else he would like, what else you can help him with, ask him for a testimonial, an opinion, etc.

Don't limit communication with the customer strictly to your sales goals, but show them that you put them first. We all feel good when we are praised and considered. It's like being done a favor that we feel obligated to return.

The ninth phase is super-loyalty, in which the customer becomes a real brand ambassador (*"What can I do to help the people at store X?"*). The power of this ambassador's voice is stronger than the entire marketing mix on which you use, in one place. This is the phase you have to aim for.

Although the stages of the sales funnel that we presented to you are similar to the traditional stages, the path that the consumer takes today is completely different. Basically, the customer is now in the driver's seat, and no matter how much brands try to impose a direction on them, they are just the passengers in the back seats.

But let's not forget that the passengers in the back can influence the travel experience and the final destination, if they have a clear map. Look, this is exactly why you need to sync your customer journey map with your sales funnel.

Remember, the customer could go through the first 6 stages of the sales funnel at the same time, or they could jump from one to another, or they could exit from any one. Because every sales funnel has holes at every step.

Instead of letting the potential client go about his business, my advice is to at least convince him to give you his contact details, but also to do remarketing for a certain period of time. Try to capitalize on every user on the site because, by having a long-term relationship, you have more chances to get the sale as well.

MARKETING + SALES = SCORE!

When you work in marketing and have to explain to someone from the outside what you do and why you do things in a certain way, comparisons are the fastest way out.

A colleague once told us how she explained what she does at the office to her husband (completely out of touch with marketing, but passionate about football). I'll use the same analogy to show you why you need to play both marketing and sales to grow your business big and profitable.

If you want to build and maintain a strong online presence, you need the combination of the two marketing schools (inbound and outbound) and a strong, interconnected sales strategy.

Basically, inbound marketing is everything that happens in your website, starting from the quality of the pages that influence the overall popularity of the website, including sales. Effective inbound marketing efforts position you more visibly in search engines, convince users to stay longer on the site and return again and again.

At the opposite pole, outbound marketing is everything that happens outside your website: presence on multiple channels, Social Media, email marketing, affiliation, link building and so on.

Now, in football terms, inbound means defence: you play on your side of the pitch, make sure you're in control and secure your goal. Outbound, on the other hand, is attacking: you play outside your zone, it's risky, but you go out to score as many goals as possible.

Even if, in the industry, we have "specialists" on each side, when they compete it is easy to realize that they are wrong.

In soccer, if you ignore defense and play only attack, you will concede too many goals - you will not win the match. And if you play hard in defense, but it seems too risky to attack, you will never score. You don't score, you don't win.

The same applies to marketing. You can invest millions of euros in PPC, Social Media and other external channels if, once on the site, the person has an execrable experience, the pages take light years to load, you have zero relevance or the content is weak. Yes, you play in attack and score goals (get goals), but they don't stay in the site, let alone come back in the future.

The same with inbound, you can build a website with a score of 10 from the point of view of usability, but it's like shouting to an empty house. Someone is needed, the users from outside, to come and live that experience of millions that the site offers. And they won't come by themselves, you have to attract them.

How do you connect with sales? Simply, think that your team (your website) is playing in the UEFA Champions League. If you want to win every match and beat your competition by getting the cup, you need game strategies for matches - campaigns, a lot of personal training, but also as a team - approaching current customers, but also new audiences, and goals - micro and macro conversions. Basically, Real Madrid or any other soccer team can teach you some great marketing and sales lessons.

Going back, the goal of marketing is to get prospects so interested in what you have to say that they drop everything else and pay attention to what you have to say. Marketing is about the market, about the problems people have, but don't want, and about the solutions they want, but don't have.

As a result, sales is about the solution product / service you sell to cover the problems.

You can make a sale only if you have convinced the prospect that one, you understand his problem, even better than he does, and two, that his life will be better, easier, more comfortable, less expensive, etc. if he will accept your solution.

If you try to sell before those two things happen, he won't listen. So the goal of selling is to demonstrate to the prospect that your solution is worth more than whatever they are paying for it (money, contact information, time, or anything else).

You may be wondering why I have written another purely theoretical chapter now, after I have also talked about the practical way. I assure you that I have also calculated this movement. Before we move on to the strategies of obtaining, optimizing and repeating the macro-conversion you are targeting - the sale, it is critical to understand that you need a unified marketing and sales strategy.

In classic large companies there are different teams for each department - and they usually fight head to head. Well, in the case of small and medium-sized online stores, the creation of specific departments or even the hiring of dedicated sales or marketing people is rarely considered.

Now, if you take care of this part yourself or have at least one person on store administration and / or sales, be sure to use the two strategies in a unified manner. You prepare the sale with marketing tactics, "warm up" leads with educational materials and sales pitches, but you're marketing to the same customers even after they've bought.

I want to draw your attention to one more thing: if you want to grow and get more sales, the budget you invest in marketing must also increase directly proportionally. I see this mistake repeated too many times in the e-commerce market - people get into a routine, invest long periods in the same marketing campaigns and surprise, they are dissatisfied because the results don't evolve, they don't get better.

Logical, isn't it? There is a finite number of individuals in the audience segment you are targeting, and if you invest in the same campaigns to get your message in front of them, their return will either remain more or less constant, or decrease. You want to reach similar markets, and when you grow you have much more varied needs and categories of audiences, therefore you have to invest little by little more as you develop.

In the following chapters you will discover what you must and what you must not do in order to reach the turnover you have targeted since the plan.

STIMULATES THE DESIRE AND PREPARES THE SALE

Our objective, of every individual entrepreneur, is to sell. The sale is the queen of conversions, and to get it, you have at your disposal dozens of tricks that you can

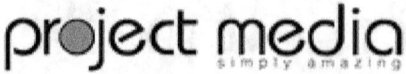

apply in your website. Some are common sense, some psychology and some traditional selling approaches updated to online and today's environment.

Here we will discuss one by one some of the most effective sales tactics, which will increase the number of orders, but also their average value - implicitly, the profit of your business: upsell, cross-sell, bundle, urgency of action and basic principles for persuasion.

The golden rules of persuasion

In his book, The Psychology of Persuasion, Robert Cialdini outlined the 6 principles of influence (I really recommend you read it). I'll show you what each of these are, with immediate applications in your online store.

1. The rule of **RECIPROCITY**
2. **COMMITMENT** rule
3. **SOCIAL PROOF** rule
4. Rule of **AUTHORITY**
5. Rule of **PLEASURE**
6. **SCARCITY** rule

First, we have the **rule of reciprocity** - give something, get something. Basically, when you do someone a small favor, say your client, they will feel obligated to return the favor. If you give them a guide or a tutorial, they will feel more motivated to make the purchase decision. Or, if you give them a small gift in the package, they will feel obliged to tell others about you/buy again.

Then comes the **rule of commitment/consistency** - when we make an official promise, we are much more likely to keep our promise. This works well in eCommerce in the order confirmation or thank you page / guide download / subscription etc. The person has already filled out a form (the order / subscription one), so the chances of them filling out another one or taking an action favorable to you (creating an account, following you on social networks, accepting an upsell, etc.) are high .

The third principle is that of **social proof** - people feel validated based on the actions of others. I have repeated this principle before: people look at what other people do and say to decide whether the purchase of the respective product is correct or not. In practice, it leverages testimonials, reviews, and marketing bookmarks (most popular product, pick of the week, best selling product, etc.).

The next rule is that of **authority** - people obey authority figures even if they are subjective (just look at the slogan *"No. 1 toothbrush brand recommended by dentists worldwide"*). In practice, think of an authority figure for your audience (celebrities, a job relevant to your target audience, industry leaders) or over time, you can become an authority name yourself. Use the image (with their consent, if it's personal names) to promote your products.

The fifth rule is that of **liking**, closely related to the halo effect - people say yes more easily when they know or like the person asking / telling them something. That's why it's so important to go to personal information on the About Us page, to display your team (with pictures) or to promote your products used by your team (or by you). For example, if you sell fishing rods, post pictures of you fishing.

The last principle in Cialdini's book is the **principle of rarity** - people are more attracted to a product if it is rarer / in limited stock / for a limited time. The truth is that this principle is the most applied by companies around the world, perhaps because it is extremely simple to use.

In your website you can use it in seasonal campaigns, discounts or to stimulate a quick decision by displaying a countdown, the number of purchases from the previous week, the number of simultaneous visitors on the same offer, the expected time for delivery, etc.

To urge action, use words such as limited time, today only, hurry, liquidation, now or never, don't delay, don't miss, offer expires in..., once in a lifetime, drop in prices, etc.

What do you have to do? To boost sales in your online store, choose one or a combination of principles and optimize your category, product and checkout pages. Add information and marketing artifice according to your chosen principles and provide a different experience for your customers.

Classic sales tactics

Now, about the sales tactics. One of the most effective is upsell - a method by which you recommend an improved product, a more advanced version of the product chosen by the customer, at a maximum price of 25% higher.

In principle, you should choose variants for upsells from the best-selling products, they should be relevant to the initially chosen option and limit the number of referrals. Display upsell recommendations early in the sales funnel (directly on the product page, after the customer has added the product to the cart, etc.). There's a maximum of 3, no need to make another mini category page in the product or cart page. My advice is to automate the whole upsell process.

Another method of increasing the value of the basket is cross-selling - you recommend complementary products for the chosen product (a shirt - a bow tie, a tie, belt; a necklace - a pair of earrings, bracelet, etc.). Basically, you provide the customer with accessories and products that go with the ordered product, so that they have the complete package.

How do you apply the tactic to your website? Clearly mark the options (*"other customers also bought"*, *"other visitors were also interested in"*, *"after a while you will also need"*, *"you may also need"*), but cross-sell on email, after the purchase has been made. To stimulate the decision, you can offer an additional benefit - a discount, faster delivery time, loyalty points, free shipping upon reaching the required value threshold, etc.

In the same vein, another sales tactic is product bundling - you give them the option from the start to buy the product together with accessories or complementary products, at a lower cost than if they would buy them separately. When choosing this tactic, pay close attention to the profit margin and always display the amount saved by the customer to demonstrate the value of the offer. Like the rest of the tactics, you can automate product bundles directly from the platform.

As a general rule, avoid cluttering the consumer's mind with too many alternatives. It minimizes the effort to make the decision by limiting the options presented, including on the home page. Yes, it's great that eMAG or Amazon can afford to list dozens of products on the front page, but remember that you are neither. User behavior and intent are different from when they enter your site.

Now, strictly for you or your team - look at every email, message or phone call from the consumer as a "who gets the most sales" challenge. Forget the "no", listen to your customer, help them (even if it means a delayed sale for you) and go hard on the upsell, cross-sell and benefits of your product versus the competition.

If you want to learn how to sell on the phone (when your customers or prospects call you), see that in the eCommerce Academy you have a great guide that has already brought results for our customers.

WHAT TO DO AND WHAT NOT TO DO WHEN THE CUSTOMER BUYS - CONVERSION RATE OPTIMIZATION

In Romania, the average conversion rate is 1%. Practically 1% of those who reach your site buy something.

The problem is that 99% of your marketing budget is going towards non-buyers and that really hurts. But these things can be improved over time.

I've said it before and I'll say it again: first marketing campaigns translate into marketing lessons, data collection, and possibly some customers.

Well, look how I slowly got to one of my favorite eCommerce topics: conversion rate optimization. This strategy goes hand-in-hand with SEO (especially technical SEO, for example if you have 404 or error pages, they prevent conversion at all) and good usability practices, and basically takes your site above all points of view.

You see, CRO tactics on their own are dead ends. That's why you need a process that combines all the elements related to the consumer experience with the testing and application of the results obtained.

So, if you were thinking of going to any agency or freelancer who does CRO by changing the size of the call-to-action button or changing something here and there, avoid them. Consider this chapter both an introduction to conversion rate optimization and a guide to choosing good CRO services.

First, let's establish some terms that you will encounter throughout the chapter. Conversion, in our industry, is the moment when the recipient of your marketing message takes an action desired by you. Subscribing to the newsletter is a conversion. Opening an email is another conversion. The fact that he follows you on Instagram is another conversion. And the purchase is the final, most important conversion.

To distinguish them, we have micro conversions and macro conversions. Naturally, small steps or minor activities performed by users lead to the final destination, the major action. But what a micro or macro conversion means for everyone is something different. For example, for a blogger macro conversion may be the moment a reader subscribes to the blog, while for an online store this is the moment of sale. You get the point.

Furthermore, the conversion rate of your store means the ratio of the number of those who complete an action on the site (buy a product, request an offer, etc.) to the number of visitors to the site. And the truth is that the resulting percentage, the overall conversion rate in eCommerce, is very low.

That is precisely why we arrive at the next term, implicitly the subject of the chapter: conversion rate optimization. This is a longer and more complex process that normally leads to higher conversion rates. The coolest thing? You don't have to invest money to bring more traffic to the site, you make it convert the existing one. Sounds good, doesn't it?

A small parenthesis: in my experience, most future entrepreneurs overload themselves by accumulating hundreds of more or less useful information for their future online store. Maybe you already have a list of a hundred optimization ideas. Well, then tell me, which one do you start with? Do you do it all at once (and your site looks like a Christmas tree)? Are you testing them one at a time (considering you'll need about 7 years or so for this)? It's really crazy.

Better yet, follow the process I'm going to describe in the following pages. Are you ready?

The formula for the conversion optimization process

The first step in creating a CRO strategy is to audit your site and analyze the data you already have. You always start here because based on this information you can form a vision of what needs to be improved, eliminated or replaced.

DATA ANALYSIS FOR CRO

I talked a little about the technical elements related to the site (what influences the consumer experience) in the SEO chapter, but it doesn't hurt to mention them here as well. To get started, log into your Analytics account and see how your site performs on every device and browser used by your visitors. Also, look at the site's loading speed - normally, if you've followed what I've told you so far, you should have a loading time of under 2 seconds.

Then, use tools to monitor behavior on the site: heatmap (follows the movement of the mouse and graphically shows you the areas of interest by color), scroll map (shows you how far people scroll on the page), click map (the places where people I click), recording video sessions of the user on the site. Deploy them with Hotjar, CrazyEgg, etc.

Don't forget that you also need direct responses from visitors. Use questionnaires on the page, questionnaires displayed when expressing the intention to leave the site, in follow-up emails and so on. You have to understand, testing will show you what a user does or doesn't do, but it won't tell you why they're behaving that way. You only get the right answer if you ask the consumer directly. You can do this through the chat application.

See how users are doing on the site, see what important elements they seem to ignore and where they get stuck. Did they ignore your call-to-action button? Maybe you need to change its size, expression or size. Do people not understand what you want to sell them? It is necessary to work on the content, to make it clearer, more concise, more descriptive. By following these aspects, you will avoid testing random things in search of the "culprit".

Centralize all this data and see what elements you need to prioritize for testing. Because optimizing the conversion rate mostly means formulating hypotheses that you test on the site over a period of time and then apply the better performing variable.

How to do A/B Testing for your store

It's like the Lottery. You only have to guess so many numbers to win the million euro prize in the Lottery. But how many people win this award in a year?

If you have 4 face-up playing cards on the table, you know that they are all SAME, basically there is a 25% chance of guessing from the first one which is the ace of clubs. Repeated attempts increase your chances of guessing the right card.

It's exactly the same with online sales. Even if things are going well the way you've done them so far and you're happy with the sales you have, it doesn't mean that this is the winning option.

By testing new scenarios and hypotheses for promoting or displaying different elements, you can greatly increase the conversion rate, generating more sales.

You see, CRO is closely related to the concept of A/B testing. Yes, it's a bit more technical because you're playing with numbers, but it's a must for increasing conversions in your online store.

Ultimate eCommerce Masterplan - Nistor Zsolt

project media

A/B Testing or split testing involves comparing two versions of pages, the original page A and page B with a single modified element, to see which one causes more conversions. You also have a second testing option, Multiple Variation Testing, where you can test more than one element per page - again to discover the variable with the best results.

If I've confused you a bit, let's get back to basics. In testing, you juggle certain aspects that it would be ideal to know before starting work:
- the element represents a unit on the page (a button, a forum mural, a block of text, etc.);
- the variable represents the different version of the page you want to
you test it (page B);
- The test represents the hypothesis that the version of an element in the varying ball will positively influence the conversion rate compared to the original page.

More clearly, you have a landing page that you want to test, so you make another variable of it with a changed element (title, image, content, etc.). You introduce them both to a similar segment of users and see which one gets the best reactions. Then you only leave the winning page live.

What can you test? What type of elements influence user behavior? Basically, you can test absolutely everything on the page, from headlines, text paragraphs, testimonials to links, images, CTA buttons, pricing structure, delivery methods, etc.

Now, look at the previously centralized data list and choose one of the most important items. It starts the process by formulating a question (for example, *"why aren't people clicking the add to cart button?"*) and formulates a hypothesis based on that question (for example, *"changing the phrase from buy now to add to cart, I will get more conversions"*).

Or *"why do people abandon shopping carts en masse"*? And you're testing displaying a more visible pop-up that lets people know that yes, the product has indeed been added to the cart, so don't forget about it.

The next step is to calculate the number of visitors per day you need to run the test. I want you to pay attention to something: avoid doing tests on a small sample (50-100 visits) because they will not be conclusive. Especially when you're just starting out and your website traffic is growing, keep in mind that in 6 months, 1 year - when the audience will be much more diverse - the results won't be as applicable. If you fall into this category, make the changes directly on the pages and delay testing until you get enough traffic.

Continuing, practically test the hypothesis by changing the call-to-action expression on the button to variable and run the test. To estimate the appropriate testing duration you can use the A/B Testing Duration Calculator from vwo.com.

Rookie Mistakes in A/B Testing

By now you've realized that any marketing action you take takes time to return results. SEO, email marketing, even PPC campaigns need a certain amount of time to bear fruit. Likewise, even more critical is this thing with A/B testing. Do you think running a test on the weekend is enough? Or for 5 days and done?

The results are enormously affected by the size of the sample on which the testing is done, but also by a number of external factors. For example, if you do tests on Black Friday or other such events, even if the results look phenomenal, I guarantee you that they are useless.

Also, run the test until you reach a safe/statistically relevant result. Don't stop at 90% but leave it until you get as close to 100% as possible. And be sure to run the test for at least 7 consecutive days because depending on the industry, there are days when users convert more or less.

Now, you may tend to roll your eyes when you see results that lead to a 3-4% increase in conversion rate, but my friend, that's not the attitude. You only get over 50% increases if your site was down before testing. Split testing helps you earn small increases, but with long-term impact, that's why you need to test constantly.

Any split test works on the basis of two components: the creative part, where you make changes based on data, not on personal preferences (you don't need to know from the start that version B will bring more conversions, because then you implement it directly) and the technique, more precisely the platforms dedicated to this tactic. Use testing tools such as Visual Website

Optimizer, Optimizely, etc. (you can try them for free before choosing one).

And please, please, don't invest precious resources and traffic to test silly aspects. You may have seen online what amazing increases x or y achieved when changing the color of the call-to-action button.

The problem is that you get stuck on little things like colors (I don't know, test the button on turquoise, on dark blue) when there are a lot of other elements that drastically influence people's experience on your site. As long as the color of the action buttons contrasts with the background and is consistent across all pages, you shouldn't have to think about it.

First, test your order flow, product page, contact page, or other commercially important pages for you, and leave the details for later.

I recommend you to split tests outside your website as well: in emails (starting with sending different subjects), in PPC ads (keywords, positioning, content, landing page), with the lead magnet, etc. It also tests by device to make sure mobile users navigate the site and have a pleasant experience.

Finally, to analyze the results, send the data to Google Analytics. Everything should be analyzed and monitored in Google Analytics. I don't know, write it down anywhere, on the bathroom mirror, on your laptop, on the ceiling, to see it every morning when you wake up. Based on the data from Analytics, you make new changes to the site and create other hypotheses that you will test.

It is possible that at first you will make mistakes, maybe it will seem quite complicated. But don't give up. Remember that before you run, always learn to walk.

Maybe you won't get conclusive results from the first test, but with patience and perseverance you will go far and propel your business to the top places in the market, where you have more visibility and more sales.

If following this optimization process you have gone from 1% to 2% conversion rate, that means you have doubled your number of orders and probably your revenue.

We have had cases in which, following this process, the value of the basket increased a lot. Because users had more confidence in the store, and the design was already much more airy.

RECOVER ABANDONED CARTS, FULL OF MONEY

But hang on, we're not done with conversion rate optimization tactics yet. One of the biggest problems in eCommerce is the problem of shopping cart abandonment. Basically, you are one click away from the sale, but the man, influenced by who knows what, chooses to leave without looking back.

And it's frustrating. The conversion is there, on the tray, in front of you, you can smell it, but you're tied hand and foot because you can't touch it. The bad news is that we currently have an overall cart abandonment rate of over 70%. The good news is that there are various ways in which you can lower the percentage as much as possible.

Abandoned cart recovery tactics fall under the conversion rate optimization process and add up to a mix of real-time marketing and reaction to user behavior. So how do you get your money out of your empty baskets?

First, you're trying to prevent churn. Show strong evidence of trust on your product, cart and checkout pages, and you should minimize the number of steps required to complete your order. It interacts personally in the cart page with the user through live triggers / push notifications in which you offer them an additional benefit if they complete the order.

CART RECOVERY SEQUENCE

If they want to leave the page anyway, show them an exit pop-up with a discount, free shipping, faster delivery time, etc. If he still doesn't want to, at least ask him for his email address or a reason why he refuses to buy from you (ask him to fill out a questionnaire).

Always get something from your potential customer. Every bit of information counts in your plan to conquer the world.

If the prevention methods did not bear fruit and the person abandoned the cart, create a strategy to recover his attention and interest. Use remarketing (works great with Facebook Ads) exactly with abandoned products and create relevant, emotional messages to drive the decision to complete the order.

You can also use an automated email sequence for cart recovery. After leaving the site, within 30 minutes at most, if you have the person's email, send them a friendly message reminding them that they left their products with you.

If the response is slow, send them an urgency-based email telling them that the products in their cart are out of stock, the cart is expiring, or they still have a chance to pick it up by a certain deadline.

Didn't get the sale after the second email? Send him a final message that you're running on a limited-time offer or discount.

You'll notice I left the discounts as a last resort, and for good reason. People have already been trained to expect a discount as soon as they abandon the cart - some do it on purpose. See if you can give him something to think about with the first emails and decide for yourself if you choose to satisfy his desire for a discount or not. Regardless of the method you choose to remind them of the abandoned cart, avoid overwhelming the user: no remarketing messages with the cart every day for 6 months, no desperate approaches. Use relevant CTA phrases and basically combine humor with urgency, because these two sensations bring the best results.

POST SALE STRATEGIES

Do you remember what it was like on your first date? Flowers, attention, conversations for hours, everything was attractive and sexy. So? Let's fast forward. You liked each other, you loved each other, and all the fun turned into something serious.

Then you got married. And maybe the messages of declarations of love or whatever you used to exchange started to be limited to "have a loaf of bread when you get home" or "do I need to get something from the store?".

Well, selling is just like a love relationship. First is the courting phase, in which both you and the client feel the ground, to convince each other of the value offered. You give him content, attract him on all channels and the moment you get married - he buys, it's a key event in your business life. The problem is that, instead of spicing up the relationship after the moment of marriage, you start to become boring with the content or get into a routine: you send him sales offers, the client ignores you.

In order for your store's relationship with the customer to last and be profitable, you need a strategy starting from the moment of purchase to loyalty and super retention - the last stage of the sales funnel that I told you about.

When making a purchase, the customer provides you with a huge collection of data - email, phone number, name, location, as well as some indicators of behavior and interests. It would be a waste on your part not to take advantage of these opportunities to continue your relationship with him.

Ultimate eCommerce Masterplan - Nistor Zsolt

project media

Okay, so it all starts the moment you get a new order notification. Imagine what's on the customer's mind right now. Without a confirmation message, an email or an SMS, all the worries before the order come back to his mind: if it's thorny, when will the order arrive, what does that product actually look like and so on.

Reassure your customer immediately by sending him an autoresponder confirming receipt of the order and telling him that you have already started preparations for sending it. Yes, even if it's 12 at night.

You can add to the branding chapter, keeping his mind occupied until he receives the package - send him an onboarding email, tell him who you are and what are the strengths of your store. In the meantime, when you prepare the package, add a personally signed card / note thanking them for their choice and inviting them to join your community.

Also here you can add product samples (if your business lends itself to such a thing), small gifts related to your business, gift coupons for him or his loved ones or you can ask him a favor - to share the moment of opening the package or pictures / video with your product on social networks, using a specific hashtag (so you can find it faster).

Remember what I said about the principle that if you ask him a favor, he'll feel obligated to return it? Sending these little attentions in the parcel works exactly on this principle.

After the package has been delivered and the customer did or did not do what you asked, send them another message and ask them how they are doing, if they are happy with the product and provide them with tutorials, how-to guides or ideas . You can also show him what he needs to do to return the product if he feels it's not ok.

Don't be afraid that the person will immediately return the product just because you told them how to do it. On the contrary, he will understand that you really want to help him and even if it is necessary to return, he will choose a less painful option for you - for example, he will choose another product instead of the original one (situations often encountered in fashion, when customers order the wrong sizes - so you can make fun of the trouble, telling them that it will be easier for them to make a return if they only ordered the product for a cool outfit at a wedding).

You can also ask him to give you a review (to facilitate the process, you can provide him with a short questionnaire), directly by email or on your Social Media pages.

Lots of people are browsing, interacting and posting on Instagram. Including your customers. Now it's simple to turn user actions into benefits for your online business.

You can ask your customers to post photos / videos of your products on their Instagram account, using a specific hashtag customized for your brand.

Then, you can display in your store, automatically, all the public Instagram posts that used that hashtag. Basically, you create a gallery of testimonials from customers who now become your brand ambassadors.

After completing these steps, you can send them product recommendations for cross-sell, upsell, product packages, but beware, customized according to the product originally ordered. This is how you create a continuous cycle that will work automatically with each new sale.

FIND OUT WHY YOUR CUSTOMERS LOVE YOU (OR NOT) - FEEDBACK

Since we were talking before about testimonials and reviews, let's take a closer look at how you can elicit reactions from customers to further use them as trust marks for your marketing strategy.

Why should the subject of testimonials stress you out? Simple, because social proof is one of the most powerful persuasive tools you could own. Sometimes they are placed directly on your tray by customers. But in most cases, you have to put in a little effort to get them.

And that's question #1: Why can't I get testimonials organically / how do I get clients to willingly give me their story?

Well, testimonials go hand in hand with the consumer experience on the site, at purchase, but also after the transaction has been completed. If you needed another reason for the after sales strategy, here's one.

Now, let's move on to some ways you can encourage feedback, as well as some best practices for getting strong testimonials. In the post-sales strategy, we have already recommended a method for surveying the customer by email, but we do not stop there.

From the beginning you should know that there are several types of reviews. What you're after are the powerful testimonials, the ones that tell stories, establish a problem or an objection and directly offer a solution. Therefore, when prospective customers read them, they can find their objections along with the motivation to overcome them.

To get this type of feedback, you need to ask 6 questions. I will give you some examples of general questions, but keep in mind that you have to adapt everything to the specifics of your business. Basically, you have to dictate to the client from the start a logical thread that he can follow, give him the opportunity to become personal and emotional, but also emphasize the happy ending - the way your product changed his life.

First of all, what did you think of when you first saw the product / what objections did you have in mind before buying our product? You ask this because, regardless of business or level of purchase, every customer has objections before they buy. Maybe it's about money, time, availability - maybe that obstacle wouldn't even have crossed your mind.

Second, after you bought the product, how did it help you / describe how you felt after buying the product?

This question basically answers the earlier objections ("*At first, it seemed too expensive, but...*").

Third question, what do you like most about our product? Now you start digging deeper. If you ask the customer to focus on several aspects of the product, he will get lost, give vague answers, but if you make him choose only one personal preference, he will give you concrete answers.

Fourth question, tell me 3 benefits you gained from the product / if you had to describe the product in 3 words, what would they be? Since you have already obtained the main benefit, you can widen the area a bit and ask for 2-3 additional benefits earned by the customer. You can opt out of providing a number, but in general it makes things easier for the customer.

Next question, would you recommend our product? If so, why? / If someone asked about the product, what would you tell them? You may think that the question is less important, but this is a matter of persuasion. When the customer recommends something, his personal integrity is at stake (see Cialdini's principle of consistency). It is vital that the person officially states that he recommends your product for reasons x, y, z.

The last question, optional, would you have anything to add to the product / would you have anything else to add? At this point, the customer has usually said all they had to say, but it doesn't hurt to ask them one last question. Basically, it's a follow-up to the previous question (which warms it up) and sometimes you can get constructive feedback or at least a stronger / personal testimonial.

I know, it seems hard and a little embarrassing to ask for testimonials straight up, but would you still do it if you didn't believe in the benefits of your product? Instead of marching on the upsell and sale as soon as the product has been bought and annoying the customer, it is better to give them a clear proof that you care about them and their happiness.

Also, when you ask for testimonials, expect unfavorable, negative responses. That's it, you can't please everyone, but it's vital to answer them right away and try to fix what's needed.

In the same vein, even if you're tempted to build your own testimonials, don't. It takes an enormous emotional detachment to build something objective and credible, instead of glorifying your product and company. Even if it's a little more difficult, be fair and create opportunities for your customers to express their own opinions.

Good, now you know what questions to ask, but how do you do it, how do you get them in front of the customers? You can formulate a questionnaire that you send in the follow-up email after the purchase, you can create an email that you send to all your existing customer base and you can stimulate the customer's decision by offering them a discount on their next order or loyalty points .

Also, tell him that his opinion will be made public on the site, but word the address in such a way that you communicate his sense of pride and self-esteem. In any case, you must obtain his consent to publish testimonials. Create an email template that you set to send automatically in the email sequence after each purchase.

So, once you get the feedback, you have to work a little to make it 100% credible. Edit your incoming texts so they have a logical structure, include photos from your customers or video testimonials, and place them strategically on your website pages, especially your sales pages.

Want another tip? Don't remove negative reviews altogether. On the one hand, even if at first they seem to hurt your business, you could get testimonials from people who like your product and services, but have a personal dissatisfaction (for example, it doesn't fit them because of a personal reason) . On the other hand, even if you mess up, the customer is unhappy and says so publicly, respond to them as soon as possible and try to reach a solution.

Also, remember that no matter what you do, there are individuals who are not comfortable with anything. Or they leave you negative reviews just for the sake of doing it. Find them, understand if their opinions are valid or not and avoid getting into polemics - washing dirty laundry is done privately.

If you have a bigger budget, you can do some endorsement campaigns by collaborating with celebrities in your field that your target audience follows. And this is a form of social proof.

CUSTOMER LOYALTY - HOW BRAND AMBASSADORS GROW

For how many years I've been working in online sales and marketing, I've noticed an interesting pattern: when purchasing from rural areas, customers recommend products further afield and buy several times from the same place - in a much larger volume than when purchasing in urban areas.

Somehow it's easy to imagine why: she sees you from the neighbors at the gate because you bought something and her curiosity pushes her to ask you what and from where. Or, if you grew up in the country, you know well how it is with the tradition of renewing the holidays and going to the neighbors to share the latest news with them.

As for the fact that they tend to remain loyal customers, in the village people are more conservative and less willing to experiment, especially when it comes to online.

These loyal customers, regardless of their background, are the ultimate goal of any business. Because, statistically speaking, it is much easier and cheaper to sell to them than to invest in attracting new customers.

Although a loyalty program is beneficial for any online business, there are some categories of businesses that have more to gain by implementing one. Basically, you earn more if you have a constant flow of orders (or at least 10 orders per month) because it automatically means that you also have someone to be loyal to, if your target audience is sensitive to price / price fluctuations, but also if you activate in a market with many competing firms.

For example, maybe competing companies don't invest in a loyalty program, and then it means that you have great opportunities to capture the attention and decision of customers. Basically, loyalty programs focus on rewarding a customer action. In other words, you give him a reward when he buys or when he does another beneficial action for you: he creates an account, shares the purchased product on social networks, gives you a testimonial and so on.

How to build a loyalty program

If on a general level, all loyalty programs are the same, the difference is the way you align the theoretical part with the specifics of your business. Here are the steps to build such a program.

First, what action is encouraged and rewarded? Mainly it's about selling, but you can also reward customers' time or effort, not just the fact that they give you money: subscription, account creation, distribution on Social Media, testimonials, content generated by them (video, images), participation in a contest and so on

Next, what type of reward do you want to offer? Think of valuable and relevant rewards for your type of customer, and if you can afford to offer them. You can offer immediate rewards (coupons and discount codes, free shipping, etc.) or/and rewards over time (loyalty points, exclusive future access, etc.) for which they have to wait. In the same vein, the third thing to think about is how the reward will reach the customer and how he will use it.

CREATE A LOYALTY PROGRAM

The next step is to set some rules for your loyalty program to avoid abuse of some users.

In principle, I recommend that you offer rewards (loyalty points) only to customers with an account, sent only to the email used to register the respective account, that they are not transferable, that they can only be used to purchase products from the website (without value in cash) and to state directly from the terms and conditions that it is your right to suspend an account at any time.

Best advice? Keep things simple. Avoid complicated regulations, which customers do not understand or find difficult to comply with. Use loyalty points whose value is equivalent to x lei and which, accumulated in a certain number, lead to receiving a gift, a discount, free shipping or any other type of benefit.

The big advantage of loyalty points is that they drive repeat purchases over time and don't affect your profit margin.

Whatever type of loyalty program you implement, always put the customer experience first. Think about what is useful for him, what he likes, what would surprise him so that he waits eagerly for every package from your store.

Don't be afraid to customize. Be inventive with the envelope or box you pack the products in (you can even print inspirational messages, a greeting, a different design on the inside) and surprise him with small gifts.

They also create separate campaigns for loyal customers. They offer preferential prices, tutorials, special seasonal offers or additional products, extended period for booking orders, preferential notifications when products are back in stock, the possibility of pre-ordering newly launched products, sending them anniversary emails on birthday / on the occasion of a shopping year or whatever suits your business.

For example, you can offer courses or organize certain events - give them preferential access. Regardless of the method chosen, make sure they are aware that they are being treated like celebrities.

Don't forget to make your program visible on all website pages (especially the front page, product page, cart and checkout) for both existing and potential customers - for which you emphasize the benefits of membership in your community .

HOW TO PUT YOUR BUSINESS ON AUTOMATIC PILOT

As an entrepreneur, in the beginning you go through everything, you start learning things, doing them, seeing what works and especially what doesn't work. This way you identify yourself where there is potential, when to give more time and budgets to grow the business.

Once these processes are identified, you realize that they can be both outsourced and automated.

Even if the people behind a business are the most important, automations have their role. And that's exactly what I'm going to tell you about.

We, in the company, have a lot of automated processes: from the welcome messages for those who choose to subscribe to our newsletter, to identifying their needs (whether they are new to eCommerce or not), to the continuation of the communication sequence.

The billing process is also automated.

The chances of errors and problems occurring are higher where there is human intervention. So I recommend that people on your team handle the really important stuff. Of those actions that bring value to your customers and that cannot be automated.

However, keep an eye on your bots. Even on days off, colleagues check incoming emails or open tickets on support, coming up with answers and solutions where necessary.

In eCommerce, first of all, you have to love what you do and want to do it beyond the financial side.

Then you have to take action. So far I have talked about a lot of more technical or less known elements for you, but believe me, it is important to know about them.

If at first you want to take care of everything, you can take the step-by-step information for implementation. And when you choose to outsource, it's good to know what can be done, where to reach, what to ask for and what to look for when you receive marketing suggestions or reports for the activities performed.

Online, we have access to more data than any god would want anyone to have. So, no wonder we feel overwhelmed and instead of making data-driven decisions, we're paralyzed.

But things can be the other way around - monitoring your business can turn into one of your favorite activities. You can be among those who have a well-structured data monitoring and enforcement model - stay away from the losers.

In this chapter, I want to show you that data can also have sex-appeal, the word comes. I want to help you simplify your life by recommending a minimum number of metrics and performance indicators to track both overall, at the site level, and for your marketing strategy

Ideally, you'll go from *"woe is me, what am I doing?!"* to *"what should I do with all the time and money I have at my disposal?"*.

Sounds good? Let's see what it's all about.

PERFORMANCE INDICATORS IN E-COMMERCE

Yes, data is important. It helps you market better. It helps you sell smarter. Blah, blah, blah.

You know the mantra well: measure, find the big picture, act. Drive yourself to sales heaven. The question is how do you do all this without losing your patience in the mess of data you see in Analytics or whatever platform you use.

In eCommerce we have hundreds of metrics. Some are generally valid, others align with business specifics, and others are little-useful, top-of-the-funnel metrics that look good and convey a sense of self-esteem, but only on the surface. Not all metrics are also performance indicators, but all indicators are metrics. Seems a bit complicated? Let's see how you make a difference.

Honestly, I just looked on Wikipedia to see the official definition of performance indicators, but it seems as confusing as Google's rules. No technical jargon and convoluted wording: KPIs are measurements that help you understand how your business is doing against set goals.

It's that simple. While you might be tempted to treat any metric as a KPI, first think about whether it's actionable and helps you reach your goal. Because it's impossible to give you a list of 100 KPIs and say *"look here, follow these and you're guaranteed to be the best"*.

The most important indicators are different for each individual business.

KPIs for small businesses

In what follows, I'll use a framework based on acquisition, behavior, and goals to recommend performance indicators based on the size of your business.

We start with the most appropriate metrics and performance indicators for small businesses. These are fragile ecosystems - people working hard to do the best with little money.

What should small businesses measure at the acquisition level: clicks, visits, backlinks, impressions? No, the most important KPI is cost per acquisition. If you fall into this category, you should be obsessed with this metric because you're on a tight budget - so you need to know what you're giving. Every action you take has a cost (not just PPC campaigns).

To identify your own cost use the following formula: total cost for marketing and sales campaigns + fees associated with marketing and sales + cost of marketing and sales programs and services / total number of customers.

What should small businesses measure at the behavioral level: pageviews, time on site? No, one of the KPIs to watch is the bounce rate or rejection rate, in Romanian. This indicator helps you identify campaigns where you are targeting poorly (so uninterested people enter the site and leave immediately) or those where you are sending relevant traffic to irrelevant or poorly tailored pages.

The second vital KPI for small businesses is cart abandonment rate - the fastest way to make money is to take it from people who have already decided to give it to you.

So, be obsessed with the abandonment rate and calculate it according to the formula: the total number of those who completed the checkout / the number of those who started the checkout. Test with A/B testing to remove barriers to the purchase decision and do smart remarketing.

What should small businesses measure at the goal level: subscription rate, revenue? No, the KPI to track is conversion rate, more precisely macro conversion.

Track the products people buy, see which traffic sources convert better. Invest more in them, improve them and create marketing strategies to attract people from these sources to the most commercial products.

These 4 indicators - cost per acquisition, bounce rate, cart abandonment rate and conversion rate are enough to get started for any small business.

KPIs for medium businesses

But what if you have an average business? In addition to the previous performance indicators, which you also need to track, you have more complex needs and metrics to monitor.

At the purchase level, in addition to the cost per purchase, it also monitors the click-through rate. If the first indicator tells you how the performance of your campaigns looks as a whole, the click-through rate allows you to analyze in more depth aspects such as the creativity and relevance of your approaches.

At the behavioral level, it additionally monitors the number of pages per session. The truth is that a small percentage of your total visitors view more than one page on your site. Look beyond average time on site and focus on page distribution, as well as the percentage of those who viewed multiple pages and converted or not.

You find a specific report in Google Analytics: Audience → Behavior → Interaction → Depth Level.

A second KPI in the behavior chapter is loyalty (number of repeat visits). If Depth helps you optimize for a single session experience, Loyalty helps you optimize for multiple sessions. For any kind of business, loyalty makes the difference between staying afloat and super profitable.

Where do you find the loyalty report? In Google Analytics: Audience → Behavior → Frequency and Recency.

At the goal level, medium-sized businesses should measure their macro conversion rate as well as their micro conversion rate. Pick any market statistic and you'll see that less than 2% of visitors convert. Focusing only on macro conversion rate would mean not caring if you can get value from the other 98% that don't convert.

You see, as Avinash Kaushik rightly says, generally sites focus on one-night stands with clients: *"Hi, nice to meet you, now take off your clothes and jump into bed with me !"*. Of course, I don't say it like that. But the *"buy now, buy, buy"* approach gives exactly the same impression.

Do you know what the problem is? Most clients don't just want a one-night stand. They want to visit your site, get informed, leave, visit other sites, come back to you, start to trust your brand more, compare prices and reviews on Google, come back to the site, add a product to cart, ask their wife/boss/friends for permission or validation, go back and buy.

So, identify micro conversions (goals) and obsess over their long- and short-term value to your business. Set goals from the start in your Google Analytics account, including their value, and to monitor them see the Conversions → Goals report, including goal URLs.

The second KPI is the goal value. This performance indicator helps you get rid of the obsession over the macro conversion rate (the 1-2% we were talking about) and allows you to create a business that delivers more than sales offers to customers.

Not all visitors convert, but ideally, each visitor will provide you with some economic value. Track this metric to identify higher-value targets and focus on those channels.

If, for example, Facebook brings you 0.50$ in value, and Google, 2-3$ or so, maybe you should focus more on SEO before making your next post.

Well, these are the main KPIs for medium-sized businesses. The difference between them and small businesses is that you need to focus on multiple conversions, detailed site interaction and advanced purchase efficiency analysis.

KPIs for big business

We're going to talk about performance indicators for large businesses, and even if you don't fall into that category yet, it's important to see what kinds of needs and metrics dictate their performance.

At the procurement level, track the sources / methods of procurement constantly. Why did I choose this indicator? Because you don't have to rest on your laurels, even if you have a large business. Obviously, there is a finite number of people to whom your products and services are relevant, but this metric helps you calibrate your marketing strategy to bring as many customers as possible to your business. Follow the report in Analytics Acquisition → All traffic volume → Source / modality.

At the behavioral level, it monitors Events. Typically, large sites deliver more complex experiences through more advanced technical tools. Too few choose to monitor the effectiveness of these technologies. That's why event tracking helps you measure expensive initiatives. Where do you find the event report? In Analytics, Behavior → Events.

The second KPI is customer value (LTV). This indicator is basically a prediction of the net value assigned for all the relationships you will have with the client in the future. What does it help you with? The idea is that it shows you how to minimize the loss rate, how to implement a loyalty program and if it needs to be optimized - it helps you make more responsible decisions. You can find the report in Analytics (Public → Customer Value) or you can calculate it yourself using the formula Average Order Value (AOV) x Net Profit % x Average Retention Time.

At the goal level, the KPI to track is time to purchase. This indicator helps you understand how fast (or slow) your visitors are converting. Because people only do a favorable action for you when they feel comfortable.

Remember what I told you earlier about the one night stand approach? The time report shows you the average number of meetings with the customer until he converts.

At a minimum, if the report shows a duration that is too long for your taste, change the messages of the marketing campaigns, draw attention to the call-to-action buttons and optimize the landing pages. Don't forget to create a strong strategy for micro conversü. If you have an online store, you can find the report in Conversions → Ecommerce → Time to purchase.

If you have a non-eCommerce site, Analytics provides you with the Multi-Channel Report (from Conversions). From there, watch the Top Paths to Conversion report - it will show you exactly the same data as for an eCommerce site.

Based on that data, it optimizes the whole process *"hello, nice to meet you, what would you like, look what I have to offer, why don't you ask your wife too, come back later, more times , I'm still here, you're ready to buy, look how...".*

You can find an additional KPI here in the Assisted Conversions report (Conversions → Multiple Channels). It's also based on the idea that people take longer to convert and interact with you on more channels before making a decision.

If the last click before the conversion came from an affiliate, should you only optimize for this conversion? Even if the visitor originally came from Google (or Facebook or whatever)?

Smart companies know that a conversion depends on several touch points and use the Assisted Conversions report to build and optimize a portfolio of profitable channels.

These are the main KPIs at a general level for large businesses, in addition to which they must also monitor the KPIs for small and medium-sized businesses.

Obviously, depending on the specifics of the business, the sales methods and a lot of other factors, you will have to monitor other performance indicators - average order value (AOV), year-on-year growth (YOY), Net Promoter Score - measures consumer experience in contact with a business (NPS), revenue flow, return rate, profit margin, best performing products and categories, etc.

What's important to remember about performance indicators is that the numbers you see in Analytics right now aren't the ones that matter most. It is vital to monitor the evolution of indicators over time, both at the site level and at the segment level - for example, the ROI of email marketing campaigns

I remember one of the test projects done on this for a client. Basically, we wanted to see the customer's brand loyalty in the cold, beyond statistics, questions and other applications.

More specifically, I made another store with the same products and different offers. With the help of PPC campaigns through Google Ads, we were able to quickly reach existing customers with advertisements.

The conclusion was that those customers who make occasional purchases of small amounts are more likely to buy from other stores, precisely because of the price. Old customers, who make more frequent purchases, with total purchases of larger amounts, are more loyal to a brand.

GOOGLE ANALYTICS - BEGINNERS GUIDE

You have created an online store. You've worked hard to get it up and running, to respond quickly to customers, and to promote your products to them. But how do you know who your most profitable customers are or how do they find you? How do you figure out what each new site visitor wants?

The answer lies in data analysis and monitoring. There are a multitude of tools on the market designed specifically to monitor the performance of websites. However, there is one tool that stands out - Google Analytics. And the truth is that Google Analytics has become the standard in the data monitoring industry today.

While I mentioned certain reports and components of a standard Analytics account in the previous chapter, I thought I'd set aside a few pages to walk you through the platform, from account creation to tips and practical examples.

You see, you might as well not monitor your online store at all. As incredible as it may seem, there are still online store owners who haven't looked even once into an Analytics account or implemented the wrong tracking code from the first, and the account is useless.

But in today's market, when any detail can make the difference between a purchase in your store or one in a competing store, Google Analytics is a must for your business.

I've had clients with years of experience behind them who didn't have an Analytics account. Or the data was corrupted due to implementation errors. Or who have never passed the Analytics platform admin panel. They came to us with 2-3 orders and grew to over 100 orders per day over time.

That's why you also need monitoring and analysis - to have a real strategy and to grow as a business, in sales and customers.

And why not use Analytics?! It's a free platform and although you have other solutions at your disposal, many of them still rely on Google Analytics to import the data needed to monitor.

Your Google Analytics Account

Imagine that you have just opened a clothing store near the center of your city. Everything is arranged, beautiful, lit, goods on the shelves, offers, mannequins, etc., but in the first days no one enters.

Then you start talking to all your friends about the store, you invite them to see your products, you also start an advertisement on the local radio, you make a few posts on Facebook and Instagram with the #hashtag the name of the city, all to bring people to the store.

After a few days you see the first customers appear and you start to rejoice because your efforts have paid off. This motivates you and you do the same actions again and again... and again and again and again.

Everything changes when you draw the line and look at costs. How much you invested in all the shares and what sales they generated. Then you think about how you can invest only in those actions that had an impact on sales.

Well, offline it is quite difficult to do such analysis, but in your online store everything is possible.

Now, I'd like to leave the theory and the pros and cons aside - what you need to know is how you can practically have a well-organized account, but also what to look for in it. Let's get started.

To create an account, you need a Google account, and once you sign up, you're guided through a series of simple steps to make the initial settings. The most important step is to implement the tracking code in all pages of your website. Many mistakes are made here, so I want to insist a little.

The tracking code must be implemented on all pages (otherwise page views are not recorded) or you limit it to your own domain (using _setDomainMethod). In the same vein, avoid duplicating code on the same page, otherwise the reports will be erroneous. After you deploy your code, make sure you've done it right by using Google Tag Assistant.

Once the implementation is complete, the program will immediately start collecting data, and in a few days you can look at the reports.

Now, before we go any further, it's important to know some basic terms to navigate the platform. In this case, it is about 2 main elements - parameters and metrics. Basically, parameters describe the data - for example, the geographical location can have parameters such as city, country, continent, etc., and the value of the parameters can be Bucharest, Cluj and so on. Parameters help you organize, segment and analyze data.

Metrics, on the other hand, measure data. These are individual elements of the parameters defined by sums or proportions. Keeping the previous example, for the Bucharest parameter, a metric can be the city's population - 1.88 million inhabitants (October 2019).

All Google Analytics reports have standard (main) parameters and metrics, but if you want more detailed reports, you will need to apply additional elements, segment the data.

Now, there are a few rules I recommend you follow. If you have an online store, it is mandatory to make the settings for e-commerce (Admin → Display → E-commerce settings) and make sure that your eCommerce platform is correctly integrated with Google Analytics.

Next, enable internal store search tracking (Admin → Display → View settings → Site search settings). Fill in the query parameter, which you find by doing a random search on your site (look at the URL, the parameter is what's between "?" and "="). Don't forget to save the setting when you're done.

Next step, create the first goal in the account to track the number of subscribers. If you have a single opt-in, you create a single goal, if it's a double opt-in, you create 2 goals / events. Add a new goal from Admin → View → Goals, name the goal (e.g. Subscribe without confirmation), select Destination and fill in the URL of the subscription thank you page (without the domain name).

Also, monitor your blog with Google Analytics. In principle, to do it you insert the code in the blog pages as well, if it is part of the domain. If the blog is on a different domain, I suggest you create a separate property just for it.

Next step, connect your Google Ads and Google Search Console accounts with Analytics (Admin → Property). Be careful to avoid tagging Ads destination URLs in Analytics, as it will overlap with Ads auto-tagging.

Once you've done this, create a new Remarketing Audience (Admin → Property → Audience Definitions → Audience segments). You can create segments for those who abandoned the shopping cart, those who viewed a specific page, those who did internal searches, loyal visitors, etc. Moreover, here you can also set dynamic attributes to run dynamic remarketing campaigns, adaptable to the interest expressed by users.

Another vital thing is to exclude internal IPs (yours and your team's) because otherwise you end up with erroneous data - numbers that look good but are actually just you and the team behind them. Create a new filter from Admin > View → Filters New Filter → Exclude → traffic from IP addresses → that are equal to and complete with your and your colleagues' addresses.

Other useful elements of your Google Analytics account are custom annotations and alerts. Annotations work like a logbook that you fill in every time you take a special action: a new marketing campaign, changes in design or content, news, etc. Thus, if there are positive or negative changes, you are aware of what caused them.

Instead, personalized alerts are automatic in Analytics and can be received by email to notify you every time there is a major change in the site: peak traffic, sudden drop in traffic, decrease or increase in the number of transactions, etc. Create alerts from Admin → View → Custom Alerts.

Reports from your account

In the platform you have several standard reports regarding the most important aspects of the business: real-time, audience, acquisition, behavior and conversions. I will now explain how to look at the data for whatever type of goal you set.

The real-time reports are some of my favorites. The idea is that you can see what the visitor is doing, where he is coming from, what he is interested in right when he is on the site. The real-time functions are super effective especially when you have a special campaign (Black Friday, other type of event) and you have to be extremely attentive to any changes.

To identify key markets and discover new markets, use audience reports. For example, the geolocation report helps you target your best visitors - the ones who convert - with PPC ads (to get your messages in front of them faster). Or another example, the demographics report is where you look when you want to make your customer avatars or update them.

From the acquisition reports you analyze the traffic sources to get more traffic to the site. Identify the main sources of traffic in the Overview report and then see in Source / way which channels you need to invest more in to gain more conversions.

In the behavior reports you find new ways to improve visitor retention and conversion rate. It's interesting to analyze the flow of user behavior because you practically learn from them what they like, what they're interested in, but also where you lose them. Or, for example, from the landing pages report you can see their performance and reduce the bounce rate, therefore increasing positions and sales.

The All Pages report helps you identify the most popular types of content and continue to invest more in them. As for the exit pages, you can immediately find the weak points of the site, make tests and changes to provide a better experience to the users.

From the conversion reports, you can make a real conversion optimization strategy. Here you can see how you are doing in terms of transactions, which are the best performing products and categories on the site, the percentage of assisted conversions, you can make comparisons between attribution models and many other actions strictly related to conversion on the site.

Another cool trick that Analytics does for you is to create a goal stream, sort of the sales funnel equivalent (provided you've set some goals).

You see, you already know that people go through a series of steps before they convert. The question is what are these steps? Are they the same as the sales funnel you built or are they following a different path? And what happens to the conversions that don't happen, where and why are you losing them? You find the answer to all these questions in the flow of objectives.

Related to the attribution model (because this is a big unknown for entrepreneurs, in general), the choice of model is conditioned by the type of marketing you do, the specifics of your business and many other factors. What is an attribution model? Basically, it's one or more rules that specify how conversions / sales are attributed to certain points in the sales funnel.

We know that during the conversion journey, the customer interacts with multiple marketing messages from you and performs multiple searches. With the attribution model, you choose how much value each touchpoint receives.

What does this thing do for you? I give you only two reasons: you can reach the conversion much faster by adjusting the contact points or you can optimize your PPC ads to the maximum with Google Ads. It can be a model based on the first click of the last visit, the first interaction, a custom model - or any other touchpoint that you think motivated the conversion. What I recommend here is not to complicate things unnecessarily, but to choose a simple model, which you understand and which is actionable.

Honestly, I don't want to go any further with Google Analytics for this book. There is a lot to discuss, a lot to learn, and for that I would need another book. The important thing to remember is that you absolutely need to monitor your site and your campaigns.

Use Google Analytics to analyze performance indicators, but also their evolution over time. Use it to identify weak points of the site and formulate hypotheses for testing and optimization, but also to make promotion decisions (for example, if you want a Black Friday campaign, analyze last year's campaign or user behavior this period last year).

Google Analytics will also show you trends and help you make better decisions for your business.

HOW TO SAVE RESOURCES THROUGH AUTOMATION

Are you still thinking about the clothes store located near the center?

In order for everything to go according to plan, you need to move quickly. When the season changes, when you bring new products, when you have stock liquidations, when you have discounts and offers, I recommend you communicate them to customers and display them in the window, so that it is as visible as possible.

And I think about how long it can take a human to check the stock daily and move the products from the shelf to the display case, from the display case to the warehouse, etc.

Clothes, like many other products, are worn with accessories and/or other clothing products that you sell.

Most of the time, the customer buys strictly what he needs. But a good sales person in the store can suggest other products that match what he is going to buy.

Moreover, that good salesman can call a customer who bought a pair of trousers after 2-3 weeks to tell him about the new offer on shirts, jackets and shoes.

Yes, it still seems like a beautiful dream - which can realistically only happen online through automations. In general, people have better and worse days, whether they feel like working or not, they have days off and vacations... during which time your business needs to keep going.

As an online business owner you are a busy man. And not in the sense of *"I have a lot of work"* but in the sense of *"if another email, a question from the client or another phone call appears in addition to the mountain of work I have to do, I'm sure going crazy"*.

It's fun to have your own business. The chances of getting bored are almost nil, and that's mainly because you don't have time left. Those who already have a business know what I mean.

You wake up in the morning and before you even get out of bed you start checking your phone, emails, enter the platform, check the status of orders, your Google Analytics account and Social Media pages.

Only then can you start your morning routine. And during the day you have to manage orders, answer e-mails and telephones, give e-mails and telephones, pack, issue invoices, solve one and another and the day ends somewhere at 10-12 o'clock at night with other checks.

That is if you work completely alone. But even if you have a team or even an employee, believe me, your tasks are reduced only to a certain extent. So how do you hold up as an entrepreneur? How do you manage to find a balance in order to have time for your personal life, for vacation or for the moments when you don't feel too well, without putting your business on hold?

The simplest and most magical answer for online is... automation. Put your repetitive tasks on autopilot with minimal involvement on your part.

Automation is beginning to be present in almost every aspect of our lives. Just think that today you can order a pizza from your phone, and have it delivered to your door in less than 30 minutes, without having to think twice.

Automation helps online businesses monitor and respond to hundreds of leads in their database without any specific person writing more than one email.

Help small businesses look like companies three times their size. And when it comes to automation, like many other aspects of your business, you need to look beyond cost.

There is a lot of misunderstanding in the market about exactly what automation means, what it is for, if it is worth it and most of all, why it is so expensive. Perhaps this is where the fear of automation comes from, because at the moment, few small and medium-sized businesses have implemented any such system.

Honestly, I personally love automations like crazy. And if you're the kind of person who has a lot on your mind, but wants to be involved in absolutely everything related to his job, I guarantee you'll love them just as much.

Unfortunately, our time is limited. Fortunately, we have exactly as much time as the planet's billionaires. And now you can use this resource in a much smarter way.

You know that the development of a business takes place over time and goes hand in hand with the actions you take during that period. Well, this is where automations help you gain speed. You can simply do a greater number of actions in a shorter period of time, eliminating manual work and the need for many human resources.

Marketing Automation

There are hundreds of definitions, formulated both by marketing specialists and even by the teams behind the respective tools, but to the point, marketing automation is the process by which you use technology to optimize, automate and measure repetitive marketing tasks.

Because you can automate any kind of marketing tactic that you have to apply at least twice: posts on Social Media channels, sending emails, browser notifications, displaying pop-ups and surveys, capturing leads, monthly reporting on competitors' activity and so on.

You see, if you want to personally do any of the actions I've listed, you find yourself with a full-time job. But you don't want something like that - you already have a job, that of an entrepreneur, and the task you have to focus on is strictly related to the relationship with the client and selling to him.

This is precisely the main advantage of marketing automation tools, it combines a suite of other tools to facilitate almost the entire promotion strategy. In this case, we have 3 categories of tools through which you can automate your activity: CRM systems, email marketing systems and marketing automation tools. Let's take them one at a time.

CRM systems (customer relationship management) capitalize on the main capital of online businesses, existing customers. Basically, you use a suite of tools and strategies to improve the relationship with customers. Typically, CRMs cover the marketing area (planning, management and measurement), the sales area (adjusting the sales funnel, managing contacts), the customer support area (centralizing customer requests, organizing employees by customer relations) and the project management area (planning, resource management, cost optimization).

I know you'd rather know what systems you could actually use, beyond the theory.

The next type of automatic tools are those of email marketing - they allow you to set up forms, autoresponders and provide you with general reports on your activity in this area. Among the tools we have tested or that you can integrate into the platform are MailChimp, Active Campaign, NewsMan, GetResponse, Conectoo, etc.

And thirdly, we have the marketing automation tools that automate your workflow: Active Campaign, Mautic, MailChimp, etc. Obviously, there are others, but I tried to limit myself to the right options for small and medium-sized businesses - advanced marketing automation systems impose (and normal) a higher cost, and we all know, cost is an extremely sensitive topic for owners of business.

Ok, how exactly do you automate?

Well, you know what marketing automation is, you wrote down some names of tools that you are going to test, now let's see how you actually do the automation. We have 3 main areas of online marketing that are well worth automating: email marketing, social media and landing pages.

The first thing to automate in your email marketing strategy is segmenting your address list based on demographics, location, interests, behavior. Using an automation tool you can create several lists by assigning tags according to the criteria I listed before. The coolest thing? You can segment people based on what interests them.

For example, you can tag subscribers according to the links they click, that is, the categories of products or content they are most interested in. Then you customize your newsletter content and emails based on those categories or content - you'll be more relevant and compelling, and the chances of them buying increase.

You can also assign tags based on the answers people give to surveys.

Next step, create email sequences triggered by set user actions. I'll just give you an example sequence, starting from the moment when the user decides to become your subscriber. It starts with a welcome email, an email to familiarize the customer with your brand. It works on the principle of "lovemarks" (from Saatchi & Saatchi) - it somehow goes beyond the brand, because a brand can be replaced after all, and lays the foundations for a much more intimate relationship between your company and the customer.

The familiarization mail, welcome, starts the personal relationship with the client, is based on a message that describes the company and basically has the role of seducing the client, making him wait for the next message from you.

Well, after the welcome email, depending on the link he clicked, behavior or interest, send him an educational email on the topic he's interested in and you can even give him a gift he doesn't expect: a guide, a video tutorial, etc. You can add a series of 1-2 educational emails. Pique her curiosity by telling her in each email when she will receive the next message and that this is another gift from you.

After you send 1-2 educational emails (every 24 hours, 2 days or you set the frequency according to your own tests) you can make him a soft sell offer, a presentation of your offer, your products. Following this email, your subscriber may or may not buy. If he doesn't, send him a hard sell offer with a time limit.

Normally, after the hard sell offer, the person should buy, but if they don't, don't get discouraged, continue with the model of 80% educational and 20%

transactional, but pay attention to the rest of the actions they take - your success it depends on the click-through rate of the mail, on noting the additional actions that the subscriber takes and many other factors.

I know it seems like a long sequence, but that's why you send it automatically, every time you gain a new subscriber. In the same idea, you can create follow-up sequences after purchase, sequences for sorting addresses from the database (with 3 reminder emails), for recovering abandoned baskets and many others. The sky's the limit for creativity, but remember to always be creative with a purpose - build sequences with a well-set commercial objective in mind.

Also regarding emails, you can differentiate yourself in the market with autoresponders that you set after the conversion takes place, regardless of whether it's filling out the contact form, creating an account in the store, etc. Sit back and think about how you would like to be assured by the store that your message was received, or what benefits you are getting for just creating an account, or any other result of the conversion you just made. you did it. That's exactly what your customers want too.

Don't give them time to come up with ideas, strike the iron while it's hot. Send them trust messages, confirmation messages, benefits, etc. as soon as they make a conversion, no matter how small, for your store.

Social Media Automation

Let's move on to how you can automate your Social Media marketing strategy. And there are two ways in which you can do the automation: one is to distribute the content on the channels and two is to increase the business on them.

You see, the average internet user has at least 4-5 social accounts (Facebook, Instagram, Twitter, Snapchat, YouTube, LinkedIn, Pinterest, etc.). You certainly have at least 2-3 accounts for your business. Well, starting to manually distribute the news (new blog articles, news, posts) is the death of passion, besides the fact that it is a time-consuming activity.

Fortunately, there are several automation tools for sharing content on social networks: Buffer, Hootsuite, SproutSocial, IFTTT, MeetEdgar, Zapier, etc. They allow you to do more than just share content en masse: schedule posting times, redistribute content or updated content, manage posts, and measure the performance of your activity on social platforms.

However, I want you to pay attention to what I am about to tell you. Automation is not always the best answer when it comes to Social Media. People catch on quickly when you take an action just to manipulate them or do it for their benefit, and at worst it can sink you into a bad image crisis.

For example, don't use autoresponders on comments, and be very careful about following accounts that use the same hashtags you're interested in - those people might be light years away from your actual target audience.

INSTEAD OF ENDING

Look, I'll be the first to admit it.

Entrepreneurship is fascinating. It's sexy. It hypnotizes you, no matter who you are, what you know, or where you come from. At the same time... she's terrifying.

Maybe you daydream about the freedom to do what you want, without anyone dictating to you, because you are already aware: you were not made to work for others.

Or maybe you're on the edge. You feel an invisible hand on your throat that squeezes harder and harder - the family must be supported, the debts must be paid, it can't be like this anymore. You try to fall asleep every night, but your eyes are glued to the ceiling as if there is a solution there. The morning finds you again with dark circles under your eyes and the hum of thoughts in your head like a rabid swarm. And you still don't know whether to do it or not.

Or maybe you want to finally have security and allow yourself to do more than just survive - you want to live, to do something important.

I can think of n reasons why you haven't taken the first step towards your first online store yet.

You don't have enough money - but I've already shown you in this book how you can succeed without investing a lot of money. And once you sell, you will have where to invest to grow.

You don't have enough time - well, I'm not getting into that because if you consider that, it means you're not ready to be an entrepreneur. Your store isn't the #1 priority on your list, so you don't have time. You have to want it, you have to want it. Think about this.

You're afraid you're going to lose. How do you know if you don't try? In any field there are risks, even in your nice and comfortable workplace where the same routine has buried you.

You are afraid of what others will say. The family. Friends. The world. Let me tell you something. Most of us who have created businesses have been pulled back by friends and family.

Because for them it seems safer, more comfortable, more like what they learned from their parents and they further from their parents - you get a secure job, get married, have children, retire, help your children and grandchildren and then you die.

It is an archaic ritual respected for generations and in which the new is very difficult to accept. But not impossible. They will judge you, yes. It is possible that at every meeting with the relatives you will be criticized for things, you will be compared to who knows what cousin who works in the administration, let's say, and how well he succeeded in life when you stress about sending the parcels on time.

Obviously, no one talks about how unhappy he feels there, or how he has a schedule as tight as the tie around his neck.

In the end, think, who will feel the greatest satisfaction? You can build an empire...but take the first step first.

All we've talked about so far is online commerce, which has virtually no borders. Even if the stories and examples given are from the experience on the Romanian market, today the word globalization is increasingly used among entrepreneurs.

Next, I assure you that once this process is understood and applied, the step towards international sales is much simpler.

About mistakes

Throughout the book I've shown you how often I've been wrong and how many failures I've faced, most of them because I, personally, have struggled.

And I did it with a purpose.

You see, what should frighten us terribly about fear is not how it makes us feel. But how they manipulate us to say NO to the things we want the most.

I want you to understand one thing. All the big companies you see now in the market, they were all just a start-up in the beginning, a small and unknown company. But they built their brand on tests, experiences, failures, mistakes and plans upon plans.

But if it were to fall now (hardly), it would be disastrous. For you, however, it wouldn't be. The earlier you are at the beginning and realize if there is potential or not, the less it hurts and the less you lose if you fail.

Something has prevented you so far from starting: the fear of risks, the fear of being judged, the fear that everything won't go according to plan... But everything doesn't have to go according to plan. It's about trying, testing, seeing what works and what doesn't, and adapting along the way. Exactly as the biggest players in the market did.

After all, now is the best time to start.

ECOMMERCE DICTIONARY

Alt Text
Short for Alternative Text which is a property of the img tag that presents a description of the image, visible when the mouse is hovered over that image or when the image is not loaded in the browser.

AIDA
Marketing Communication Model for Sales. It comes from Attention, Interest, Desire and Action.

Dofollow and nofollow attributes
HTML attributes that inform search engines that the link should influence the ranking in the index, respectively not influence it.

B2B

In eCommerce, B2B refers to the exchange of products and services between 2 businesses. It is a situation in which a company makes commercial transactions with another company. It can be manufacturer - distributor, distributor - seller, etc.

B2C

Transactions are made directly between a company and a consumer who is also the final user of the purchased product / service.

Backlinks

Link from other pages or sites sent to your main page or domain.

Breadcrumbs

A form of navigating through a website that shows the link structure hierarchically. Inside the site, the current location is indicated by a chain of links that are hierarchically structured starting from the main page (home page). Such a chain of links looks like this: Home > Products > Teas > Green tea.

Bounce rate / rejection rate

The bounce rate you have on your website refers to the percentage of people who arrive on the landing page and leave immediately, without reading your content, filling out forms or clicking on the displayed call-to-action button.

Broken links

Links within a website that when accessed open a new page containing certain errors.

Bundling
Sales technique where two or more products are bundled together and sold as such. Usually, a bundle is sold at a lower price than the total price of the products if they were sold separately.

Buyer Persona
A semi-fictional representation of the ideal potential customer, created based on a process of documenting existing customer data. Includes specific data, demographics, interests, behavior, objections, goals and so on.

Call-to-action
Expression used to urge people to do a certain action. It is found on the buttons displayed on the page (buy, add to cart, submit, etc.), it can be anchor text for a link or a text call to action to drive the purchase decision / action.

SSL certificate
Cryptographic protocol that has the role of securing the exchange of information on the net (bank cards, passwords, email, any private information).

Click through

The process of clicking on a link that appears in the page of results returned by a search engine, thus visiting the site indexed by the engine. This link is an important one because through it visitors from search engines are received on the site.

Price comparator

Site specialized in the comparative presentation of prices for products / services from the portfolios of online stores registered in the comparator.

Evergreen content

Type of content that is always valid, sustainable, relevant and useful indefinitely. In SEO it refers to content that stays fresh, always updated, for readers.

Cornerstone content

Super basic content that you send both backlinks and internal links to. Ideally, it's valuable content that provides relevant information, optimized with meta title, meta description, semantic keywords, long tail, subtitles, includes optimized images, videos, etc., and can be linked to a product page / page of category in your store.

Acquisition cost (AC)

The cost associated with attracting and convincing a potential customer. It helps you figure out how to budget better or allocate the budget to the processes with the strongest impact on your future customers.

CRM (Customer Relationship Management)
Set of tools, procedures and strategies aimed at improving the relationship with customers: customer history, interactions with the customer, management of business relationships with other companies, data centralization.

Customer Lifetime Value (CLV / LTV)
A prediction of the total value (total net profit) you will earn over the lifetime of your customer relationship, as long as they are your customer.

Responsive design
A combination of flexible grids, flexible images and Media Queries that allow the website to adapt to any device. Basically, the design responds to the characteristics of each device through which a website is accessed.

Drop shipping
Type of trade in which the goods sold are delivered directly by the supplier / manufacturer to the final customer. You, as an intermediary trader, have the advantage that you no longer have to own your own stock.

Duplicate Content Web pages distinct in design but with nearly the same content.

Ultimate eCommerce Masterplan - Nistor Zsolt

e-Fulfillment
Service that outsources the entire order fulfillment process: storage, order picking, packing and delivery. Example of e-fulfillment in Romania: Frisbo, Fulfill.ro.

ERP
Software platform that your company uses to manage activities such as accounting, procurement, project management, risk management and compliance.

FOMO (Fear of missing out)
People's constant worry that they are missing out on better alternatives and others seem to have nicer experiences, more satisfying relationships, etc. than them.

Google juice
The quality, strength, or advantage that a site acquires by ranking on the first pages of results provided by Google.

Growth Hacking
Marketing techniques aimed exclusively at growth, by finding creative means that you can use to reach customers and speed up the company's growth process.

Keyword
Word that is part of the text / expression used in the search.

Inbound Marketing

Marketing method that uses content marketing, social media marketing and SEO to attract qualified prospects and create credibility for a business. Focus on the consumer experience.

Infographic

Visual presentation of key information that uses illustrations to display content. They shorten complex information so that the consumer can understand it more easily.

Landing page

At a general level, a landing page is basically any web page on which the user can reach or "land". In terms of marketing and advertising, a landing page is a web page distinct from the rest of the site, with a special design created to achieve a set purpose: sale, subscription, data collection, event registration, etc.

Link Anchor Text / Anchor Text

The visible text of a link.

Logistics

The activities that are done to move the goods from the producer to the final customer: transport, storage, distribution.

Affiliate marketing

A strategy based on performance and cost per action (CPA). The advertiser (you), gets other people (affiliates) to talk about your products and drive traffic to your site. In return, for every sale / contract concluded with a customer who came through the link from the affiliate, you pay him a commission.

Marketplace

Entity / site that lists the products, services and offers of registered partners in front of a massive audience, for a specific sales commission.

Profit margin

How much money did you make for yourself, for the company. It is calculated according to the formula: (sale price - purchase price) / sale price.

Metas or meta tags

HTML elements inserted into website code to provide information or instructions.

Assignment model

A rule or set of rules that shows how a sale or conversion is assigned to certain points in the paths to conversion. For example, in the case of Last interaction the sale is attributed to the last clicks that preceded it.

Multichannel

Ultimate eCommerce Masterplan - Nistor Zsolt

Marketing strategy based on multiple channels to communicate a message to the customer as quickly as possible through the maximum number of individual communication channels.

MVP (Minimum Viable Product)
Product prototype. Initial product release that allows the team to validate knowledge of customers and their needs with minimal effort.

Omnichannel
Marketing strategy based on the integration and management of channels in a unified way, leading to continuity in the consumer experience, regardless of the channels through which he has contact with your company.

Organic (traffic)
Traffic resulting from a search in a search engine and choosing one of the displayed sites.

Page views
Each time a visitor accesses a web page, this visit is counted as a "page view", even if the same visitor enters the same page 5 minutes later.

Churn rate
The percentage of customers or subscribers who abandon your company or services in a given period of time. In other words, it's the profit or customers lost in a

given period by them abandoning, unsubscribing or returning your products.

Engagement rate
Metric that measures the level of engagement that a material / content receives from the audience. It shows how much people interact with that material.

301 redirect
Permanent redirection of an old URL to a new one, so that people who click on the old page are automatically taken to the new one.

Relevance
The degree to which the content of a web page returned by a search engine matches the key phrase for which the query was made.

Return on Investment (ROI)
Investment recovery rate = (Income from the investment - Amount invested) * 100 / Amount invested.

Robots.txt
File that tells search engine bots what they can or cannot access on a site.

SaaS (Software as a Service)
A system whereby the provider provides you with an internally hosted service in the cloud (e.g. eCommerce platform) against a monthly / annual subscription.

SERP - (Search Engine Result Page)
Search engine results page

Spider, Spyder
The part of the search engine that handles web browsing, collecting the urls and indexing the keywords and text of each page it finds. The act of browsing, collecting and indexing keywords is called spidering.

UI - User Interface
It represents all the aspects with which the user interacts when browsing the site; the elements that the user will use.

Unique visitor
A real site visitor. The web server logs the IP address of each visitor to determine their actual number. If someone visits 20 pages of the site, the server will count a single visitor (because the pages visited are associated with the same IP address), but it will count 20 pages accessed.

URL Specifies the web address of a file, in this case the addresses of your pages.

UX - User Experience
All the things on the site that lead to a good experience; what the user feels when using the site.

www.ingramcontent.com/pod-product-compliance
Lightning Source LLC
Chambersburg PA
CBHW052342220526
45465CB00003BA/919